TENNESSEE
Hometown Cookbook

TENNESSEE
Hometown Cookbook

BY Sheila Simmons AND Kent Whitaker

Great American Publishers
www.GreatAmericanPublishers.com
TOLL-FREE 1.888.854.5954

Great American Publishers
P. O. Box 1305 • Kosciusko, MS 39090
TOLL-FREE 1.888.854.5954 • www.GreatAmericanPublishers.com

ISBN 978-0-9779053-2-4 (0-9779053-2-2)

10 9 8 7 6 5 4 3 2

by Sheila Simmons & Kent Whitaker

Designed by Sheila Simmons

Front cover photos:
Beale Street: ©Performa Entertainment www.bealestreet.com • Guitar: ©John Murphy
www.istockphoto.com • Mill: ©Marianne Venegoni • Food: ©Renee Comet Photography, Inc.
Beale Street Barbecue Ribs p118, Roasted Cheddar Potatoes p72, Pepper & Corn Salsa p13

Back cover photos:
Pie: ©Dan Brandenburg • Tomato: ©Aerial Innovations of Tennessee, Inc. www.flytenn.com

Chapter opening photos:
istockphoto.com: Appetizers p9 © Dragan Trifunovic • Breads p23 © Thomas Perkins • Salads
p43 © Kelly Cline • Soups, Stews, Chili, & Chowders p55 © Thomas Perkins • Vegetables &
Other Side Dishes p71 © Diane Diederich • Pork p109 © Karin Lau • Beef p131 © Carol Gering
• Fish & Seafood p 165 © Suzanne Tucker • Cookies & Candies p183 © Jim Jurica • Cakes p197
© Jim Jurica • shutterstock.com: Pies & Other Desserts p213 © giordano borghi • Index
p227 © Jeff Kinsey • Crockpot, Casserole & One-Skillet Dishes p93 © Chris Dortch. Image from
BigStockPhoto.com • Poultry p149 © Paul Clarke. Image from BigStockPhoto.com

Tennessee

Contents

Hometown Cookbook

Tennessee

Introduction

Tennessee brings to mind music and mountains, history and heritage, great food and family. It is our desire to bring you a taste of it all within the pages of *Tennessee Hometown Cookbook*.

The Volunteer State has much to offer residents and visitors alike. Music is an important part of Tennessee culture—from traditional mountain music of the Appalachians in East Tennessee to Nashville's Country Music Hall of Fame and on to Memphis for some Beale Street Blues. The opportunity for outdoor recreation abounds with mountain hiking trails, national parks, camping, rivers, streams and lakes. Nowhere is the history of Tennessee more apparent than Chattanooga—five major battles of the Civil War were fought in the area of Lookout Mountain.

When the outdoor fun is done, a favorite gathering place for Tennessee friends and family is the kitchen. Tennessee's food heritage is strong... from **Country Yeast Biscuits** to **Grandma's Onion Soup Meatloaf**, **Country-Fried Okra** to **Old-Fashioned Strawberry Shortcake**... great-tasting traditional Southern food is served up on tables across the state. Throughout the generations, recipes have evolved using new and convenient ingredients and methods... we bring you **Easy Red Velvet Cake, Crockpot Chicken & Dumplings, Sunday Brunch Monkey Bread** and **Easy Tater Tot Casserole**. You'll find recipes using hometown favorite products—**MoonPie Vanilla Pudding, Goo Goo Ice Cream Stack**, and **Double Cola Barbecue Sauce**. And, if that's not enough, you are sure to enjoy such delicious recipes as **Pineapple Porterhouse & Jumbo Shrimp with Island Butter, Green Beans and Ham**, and **Caramel Pound Cake**.

Music, mountains, history, heritage, food and family all come together during the many festivals that are held throughout Tennessee each year. And throughout this book, you'll enjoy information about fun, food-related festivals. From the Lauderdale County Tomato Festival in Ripley to the Shady Valley Cranberry Festival from the World's Biggest Fish Fry in Paris to South Pittsburg's National Cornbread Festival, there's a celebration to suit every taste.

This book would not be possible without the generous support of numerous people. We spoke to many good, friendly Tennessee folks with festivals across the state and in all cases we found people helpful and generous with their time. Our gratitude goes to Annette Goode and Wendy Musgrove who are forever working tirelessly behind the scenes and Lisa Flynt for her early help with the book. A big thank you goes to our families for their unwavering support; Ally and Macee, Roger, Ryan, and Nicholas—we couldn't do it without you.

Tennessee Hometown Cookbook is for Tennessee residents, visitors, transplanted natives or anyone who wants to experience the uniqueness of the Volunteer state. We hope you will agree this is an outstanding collection of the best recipes that Tennessee has to offer... and that's saying a lot!

Wishing you many happy kitchen memories,

Sheila Simmons & Kent Whitaker

Appetizers

Mexicorn Dip

2 (11-ounce) cans Mexicorn
1 (11-ounce) can white corn
1 (4-ounce) can chopped green chilies
1 cup grated sharp Cheddar cheese
½ cup sour cream
¼ cup mayonnaise
1 teaspoon Cajun seasoning (or to taste)
1 teaspoon garlic salt (or to taste)

Drain all 3 cans of corn and green chilies in a strainer. In a large bowl or your serving dish, mix drained ingredients with remaining ingredients. Chill 1 hour or overnight. Serve with big corn chips or tortilla chips for dipping.

Hot Tamale Dip

2 (15-ounce) cans tamales
1 (16-ounce) can chili without beans
1 (8-ounce) jar salsa
16 ounces Velveeta cheese

Pour tamales with juice into crockpot; chop tamales in small pieces. Add remaining ingredients. Heat until cheese is completely melted, stirring frequently. Keep warm on lowest setting and serve with chips for dipping.

Tex Mex Dip

1 can whole kernel corn, drained
1 can black beans, drained
⅓ cup Italian dressing
1 can chopped tomatoes and green chilies
½ teaspoon cilantro
½ teaspoon cumin powder

Combine all ingredients; chill.

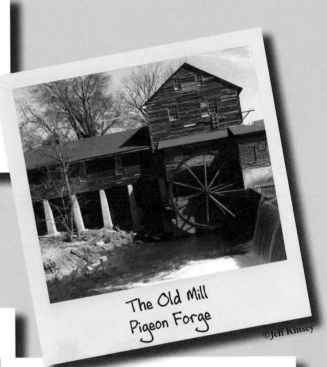

The Old Mill
Pigeon Forge
©Jeff Kinsey

Salsa Cheese Dip

½ pound ground beef, browned and drained
½ pound processed cheese, cubed
1 can black beans, drained
1 can diced tomatoes and chilies
2 tablespoons hot sauce
1 tablespoon black pepper
1 tablespoon cumin powder
½ tablespoon salt
Garlic powder to taste

Combine all ingredients; warm in saucepan to melt cheese. Serve from crockpot or chafing dish to keep warm.

Saucy Salsa

1 can tomato sauce
1 large onion, chopped
1 green bell pepper, chopped
1 can diced tomato, drained
1 teaspoon cumin powder
1 packet taco seasoning
2 tablespoons minced jalapeño peppers

Mix everything together in a bowl, cover and refrigerate a few hours before serving.

Lauderdale County Tomato Festival
Ripley • July

The Lauderdale County Tomato Festival is held every July in Ripley. Events include tomato tasting, tomato contest, gospel music, baby crawling contest and more.

www.lctn.com/tomato-festival

© Tischenko Irina

Salsa Supreme

2 cans diced tomatoes, drained
2 small onions, diced
1 small can whole kernel corn
1 bell pepper, diced
1 small banana pepper, diced
1 tablespoon minced garlic
2 teaspoons cumin powder
2 teaspoons black pepper
1 teaspoon salt
1 teaspoon sugar
½ tablespoon vinegar

Mix everything together in a large saucepan. Bring slowly to a boil. Boil gently 10 minutes. Serve warm or cooled with chips.

Pepper & Corn Salsa

2 cans diced tomatoes, drained
1 can whole kernel corn, drained
1 white onion, chopped
1 red bell pepper, chopped
1 green bell pepper, chopped
2 to 3 jalapeño peppers, minced
2 tablespoons chopped cilantro
½ tablespoon garlic powder
1 tablespoon red wine vinegar
1 tablespoon cumin powder
1 tablespoon chili powder
½ tablespoon paprika

Combine all ingredients at least 1 day before serving; refrigerate until ready to use. Will keep in refrigerator 5 to 8 days.

Shrimp & Bacon Dip

1 (8-ounce) container sour cream
1 (8-ounce) package cream cheese, softened
1 cup tiny shrimp, drained, cooked and peeled
½ cup real bacon bits
¼ cup finely chopped green onions
1 tablespoon soy sauce
½ tablespoon yellow mustard

Mix all ingredients until well blended. Chill and serve with corn chips, party crackers or vegetables for dipping.

Avocado Dip

1 pound shredded Colby cheese
2 cans chopped green chilies
2 shallots, finely chopped
2 avocados, mashed
Salt and pepper to taste
1 tablespoon olive oil
1 tablespoon vinegar
Parsley for garnish

In a bowl, combine all ingredients except parsley; chill. Top with parsley before serving.

Crab Dip

½ cup mayonnaise
1 (8-ounce) package cream cheese, softened
2 teaspoons lemon juice
1 teaspoon Worcestershire sauce
½ teaspoon Italian seasoning
½ pound crabmeat or imitation crabmeat, chopped
½ cup bacon bits
Milk

In a saucepan over low heat, combine mayo and cream cheese until well blended and smooth. Add lemon juice, Worcestershire, Italian seasoning, crabmeat and bacon bits. Continue to cook over low heat until smooth; add milk if/as needed to thin to dipping consistency. Serve warm.

Tennessee

Creamy Spinach Dip

1 package chopped spinach,
  well drained
1 cup mayonnaise
1 cup sour cream
¼ cup Parmesan cheese
1 package ranch dressing mix

Combine all ingredients in a bowl and mix well. Chill before serving.

Parmesan Caraway Appetizers

¼ cup butter
1 cup grated Parmesan cheese
1 cup self-rising flour
1 cup sour cream
1 tablespoon caraway seeds
1 egg white

These are equally good made with sesame seeds and make good dippers for Spinach Dip.

Cream butter. Add cheese, flour, sour cream and seeds; blend into a soft dough. Roll dough on lightly floured board to ⅛-inch thick. Cut into diamond shapes. (A pizza cutter works best.) Beat egg white and brush onto appetizers. Place appetizers on greased baking sheet and bake 12 to 15 minutes at 350°.

Note: After cutting dough, if it is too soft to easily lift, place in freezer approximately 5 minutes.

Cranberry Dip

1 (8-ounce) package cream
    cheese, softened
2 tablespoons sour cream
2 tablespoons orange juice
⅛ teaspoon cinnamon
1 tablespoon sugar
¼ cup chopped pecans
¼ cup finely chopped dried cranberries

Combine cream cheese, sour cream, juice, cinnamon and sugar with mixer on medium until smooth. Fold in pecans and cranberries by hand. Chill before serving with Triscuits, melba toast or other dipper.

Veggie Dip

¾ cup cottage cheese
1 package ranch dressing mix
4 ounces cream cheese, softened
¾ cup sour cream
3 tablespoons water

Beat cottage cheese on high 1 to 2 minutes, until smooth and creamy. Add remaining ingredients. Beat on medium until well blended. Chill before serving.

Carillon Bell Towers at Bicentennial Mall
Nashville
©D. Wagner

Cream of Broccoli Dip

10 ounces frozen chopped broccoli
2 cans cream of chicken soup
¼ cup milk
1 clove garlic, minced
3 cups shredded white American cheese
1 can chopped green chilies or freshly-cut peppers

Break broccoli into very small pieces. Cook in saucepan according to package directions; drain. Add soup, milk, garlic, cheese, and green chilies. Cook, stirring continuously, until cheese is melted. Serve warm.

Ham and Cheese Ball

4 ounces ham, chopped
2 (8-ounce) packages cream cheese, softened
1 cup shredded Cheddar cheese
4 green onions, chopped
1 (4-ounce) can mushrooms, chopped and drained

Set ½ of the chopped ham aside. Mix remaining ingredients together well. Roll into a ball. Press reserved ham onto ball, covering entire surface. Chill. Serve with crackers.

Bacon-Wrapped Water Chestnuts

1 pound bacon
4 cans whole water chestnuts
⅓ cup soy sauce
½ cup brown sugar

Cut bacon in halves or thirds depending on width of chestnuts. Wrap a strip of bacon around a water chestnut and insert a flat toothpick through the bacon and water chestnut. Continue wrapping water chestnuts with bacon until finished and place on broiler pan. Combine soy sauce and brown sugar in a small bowl. Spoon a small amount of sauce over each allowing it to flow down. (Do not dip chestnuts with raw bacon into sauce.) Save remaining sauce. Cook at 350° until bacon is crisp. Spoon each chestnut with sauce until well coated. Serve hot.

Pineapple Chicken & Shrimp Bites

24 jumbo shrimp, deveined and tails removed
1 (46-ounce) can pineapple juice
12 chicken tenders, halved
3 tablespoons brown sugar
2 to 3 cups coconut

Marinate shrimp in pineapple juice with brown sugar. Place one piece of chicken and one piece of shrimp on a wooden toothpick. Roll in coconut. Place 1 inch apart on nonstick pan. Bake at 400°, turning as needed, until chicken juices run clear, shrimp turns white, and edges brown. Serve hot, sprinkled with additional coconut if desired.

Mini Spinach Pastries

1 can chopped spinach, drained
1 (8-ounce) package cream cheese, softened
½ cup bacon bits
½ cup minced onion
1 egg, beaten
Mini flaky pastry pie shells

Squeeze excess liquid from spinach and break large pieces into small pieces. Combine all ingredients and spoon equal amounts into mini pastries. Bake at 350° until bubbly and brown on top.

Nashville Skyline

© Joy Miller

Mushroom Meatballs

2 pounds frozen meatballs
2 cans cream of mushroom soup

In a glass baking dish, combine meatballs and soup. Stir to evenly coat meatballs. Cover with foil and bake at 350° 20 minutes. Remove foil and bake an additional 10 minutes. Stir if needed. Serve hot with toothpicks.

So simple yet so delicious, your guests will think you slaved over this dish.

Hobo Sausage Kabobs

1 pound smoked sausage, chunked
1 package hot dogs, chunked
1 onion, thickly sliced
1 green bell pepper, thickly sliced
1 bottle barbecue sauce
Toothpicks

Combine all ingredients in a large bowl and evenly coat with sauce. On a toothpick, place 1 piece of sausage, one slice of onion, 1 piece of hot dog, and 1 slice of pepper. Repeat until all ingredients are used. Bake on a nonstick cookie sheet at 400° for about 15 minutes or until sauce and edges brown. Serve warm.

Veggies and White Cheese Sauce

½ pound white American cheese
⅓ cup milk
2 tablespoons sour cream
1 teaspoon minced garlic
1 teaspoon chili powder
Assorted veggies such as carrots, celery, broccoli, and/or your favorites

Combine first 5 ingredients in a saucepan and cook over low heat until cheese melts. Serve with vegetables for dipping.

Volunteer Ham Cubes

4 (¾-inch) deli ham slices
½ cup butter
⅓ cup brown sugar
¼ cup maple syrup

Cut deli ham slices into cubes. In a skillet, combine butter, brown sugar and maple syrup. Stir in ham. Slowly warm skillet to melt butter. Stir until ham is evenly coated. As edges begin to brown, remove from heat and place on a serving dish with a toothpicks.

Cook these just before the game and serve with a variety of cubed cheeses.

Fried Mushrooms

2 to 3 cups medium whole mushrooms, cleaned
1 cup milk
1 egg, beaten
Salt and pepper
1 cup cornmeal
½ cup crushed pretzels

Rinse and clean mushrooms. In a bowl, combine milk and beaten egg with a large dash of salt and pepper. In a separate bowl combine cornmeal and crushed pretzels. Dip mushrooms in milk mixture then roll in cornmeal mixture. Drop in hot oil and cook until golden.

Hot Cream Cheese Poppers

2 (8-ounce) packages cream cheese, softened
⅓ cup shredded cheese
2 tablespoons hot sauce
1 teaspoon minced garlic
1 teaspoon citrus jelly
2 tablespoons parsley
Melba toast
Sliced jalapeños

Combine all ingredients, except toast and peppers, in a bowl. Form into small balls and place on toast or crackers. With a spoon, press ball down onto cracker leaving an indention in the middle. In the indention place 1 pepper slice.

Chocolate Fondue Appetizers

1 angel food cake, 1-inch cubes
1 pound cake, 1-inch cubes
2 cups sliced peeled apples
2 pints sliced strawberries
2 cups pineapple chunks
2 pounds grated chocolate candy bars
1 cup whipping cream
¼ cup hot water
2 teaspoons vanilla

Arrange cake cubes on a serving plate with fruits. Melt chocolate over very low heat, stirring constantly. Stir in whipping cream as chocolate melts. Add water as needed. Stir in vanilla. Serve in a fondue pot with skewers for dipping cake and fruit into melted chocolate.

Breads

Sweet Buttermilk Cornbread Muffins

1⅔ cups self-rising cornmeal
⅓ cup self-rising flour
2 eggs
¾ cups buttermilk
¼ cup honey
1 teaspoon sugar

Combine all ingredients in a bowl and mix well. Pour into well-greased muffin pan, cornbread mold, or loaf pan. Batter will rise, so don't over-fill. Bake at 375° until golden brown, about 25 minutes.

Mr. Cook comes by often. One of the topics we always seem to chat about is bread—he owns a chain of specialty bakery restaurants, Panera Bread, as well a grocery store with a great deli. I asked him what he would consider to be the Southern Appalachian area's most traditional bread. "That's easy," he said. "Cornbread."

Hot Water Fried Cornbread

1½ cups white cornmeal
1 teaspoon salt
1 cup boiling water
2 tablespoons bacon grease
½ cup shortening or vegetable oil for frying

In a bowl, combine cornmeal and salt. Add boiling hot water and bacon grease; stir. Heat iron or nonstick skillet; add 3 to 4 tablespoons oil. Use a heaping tablespoon to pour batter in hot oil in the shape of round disks; flatten cornbread disks as they fry. Fry until crisp and brown, about 5 minutes.

National Cornbread Festival

South Pittsburg • April

Amateur chefs from all over the country compete for honors in the National Cornbread Cook-Off. Main dish cornbread dishes are eligible in this annual contest sponsored by Martha White Flour and Lodge Cast Iron. A 4-H version of the contest is open to fourth-grade 4-H'ers. Prior winners of the Cook-Offs have come from North Carolina and Kentucky to Nebraska and Wisconsin.

www.nationalcornbread.com

©National Cornbread Festival

Bacon Cornbread

1¾ cups self-rising cornmeal
1 teaspoon salt
2 tablespoons bacon grease
1 cup boiling water
½ cup bacon bits
½ cup shredded cheese

Combine all ingredients in a bowl. Mixture should be thick. Pour in greased iron skillet. Bake at 350° until top is golden brown, about 30 minutes.

Cornbread

2½ cups cornmeal
1 cup self-rising flour
2 cups buttermilk
1 cup water
2 eggs
6 tablespoons sugar
1 tablespoon salt
1 cup shortening, melted or ⅔ cup oil

Combine all ingredients. Pour into a cornbread mold or muffin pan. Bake in a brick oven, smoker, or oven at 400° about 30 minutes.

Breakfast Orange Honey Muffins

1 cup whole-wheat flour
3 teaspoons baking powder
½ teaspoon salt
½ teaspoon baking soda
1 cup rolled oats, uncooked
⅓ cup honey
1 egg
3 tablespoons oil
1 cup orange juice
1 to 2 teaspoons grated orange peel

Mix flour, baking powder, salt, and baking soda. Stir in oats. Combine honey, egg, oil and juice. Add to flour mixture. Beat until well blended. Add grated peel and stir until just mixed. Batter is thinner than normal muffins. Fill well-greased muffin tins ⅔ full. Bake 15 minutes at 425°.

Corn Biscuits

2 cups self-rising flour
⅓ cup self-rising cornmeal
1 can whole-kernel corn
2 eggs, beaten
1 cup milk

Combine all ingredients. Add more flour or milk as needed depending on whether you choose to drop with a spoon onto greased cookie sheet, cut as regular biscuits or cook in greased muffin pan. Bake 10 to 15 minutes at 375°.

Tennessee

Country Yeast Biscuits

1 (¼-ounce) package active dry yeast
5 cups all-purpose flour
1 teaspoon baking powder
1 teaspoon salt
1 teaspoon soda
3 tablespoons sugar
¾ cup shortening
2 cups buttermilk

Dissolve yeast in ¼ cup warm water. Sift dry ingredients together. Cut in shortening until mixed. Add buttermilk and yeast. Work together until flour is moistened. Cover bowl and refrigerate until ready to use. Roll-out on floured board to ½-inch thickness; use additional flour only if necessary. Cut with biscuit cutter and place onto greased baking sheet. Bake 20 to 25 minutes at 400° or until golden brown.

Yogurt Biscuits

1 cup all-purpose flour
¼ teaspoon salt
1½ teaspoons baking powder
⅛ teaspoon baking soda
2 tablespoons margarine
½ cup plain yogurt
½ teaspoon honey

Combine flour, salt, baking powder and baking soda; cut in margarine. Add yogurt and honey; mix well. Turn dough onto lightly floured surface. Knead gently, then roll and cut into biscuits. Bake 20 to 25 minutes at 375°.

Quick Biscuits

2 cups self-rising flour
¼ cup margarine, softened
½ cup milk
Dash salt
Large dash sugar
Melted butter (optional)

Combine all ingredients, except melted butter, and pat to ½-inch thickness. Cut with cookie cutter or floured small glass. Place on greased cookie sheet and bake at 400° for about 15 minutes. Top with additional melted butter last 3 minutes of baking if desired.

Ham & Cheese Biscuits

2 cups self-rising flour
½ cup shredded jack cheese
¾ cup chopped ham
1 teaspoon salt
1 teaspoon brown sugar
⅔ cup milk
⅓ cup vegetable oil
½ teaspoon yellow mustard (optional)

Combine all ingredients and knead gently. Pat dough out to about ½-inch thickness. Cut biscuits with a floured biscuit cutter. Bake on greased cookie sheet at 350° for 20 to 25 minutes.

Civil War Cannon
Lookout Mountain

©James Becker

Tennessee

Sweet Creamed-Corn Spoonbread

2 cups self-rising flour
1 can cream-style corn
1 tablespoon sugar or brown sugar
2 eggs
¾ cup milk

Preheat oven to 400°. Lightly grease a cookie sheet. Mix flour, corn and sugar. In a separate bowl, beat eggs then add milk. Mix well; add to corn mixture. Stir just until moistened. Drop by tablespoons onto cookie sheet; bake until golden brown, about 15 minutes.

Yeast Rolls

2¼ cups all-purpose flour
3 tablespoons sugar
1 teaspoon salt
1 (¼-ounce) package active dry yeast
1 egg, beaten
2 heaping tablespoons shortening
Vegetable oil

In a bowl, combine flour, sugar and salt; mix well. Boil ¾ cup water in a saucepan; allow to cool until bubbles stop then add yeast. Add to dry ingredients along with egg and shortening. Quickly mix well. Form into a ball and rub with oil. Place in a large bowl, cover with plastic wrap and allow to rise for about 1 hour or until double in size. Break dough into 10 equal pieces, form each into balls and place into well-greased muffin pan. Cover very tightly with plastic wrap and allow to rise again. Bake in a preheated 425° oven for about 15 minutes or until rolls are golden brown. Serve hot with butter.

Mayo Rolls

2 cups self-rising flour
1 cup milk
4 tablespoons mayonnaise

Combine all ingredients. If too dry, add water or oil by teaspoonful until desired consistency is reached. Roll equal amounts into smooth balls. (Do not squeeze or knead too much.) Place on greased cookie sheet or in greased muffin pan. Bake in a 350° oven 10 to 12 minutes.

Homemade Wheat Rolls

7 cups wheat flour, divided
¾ cup sugar
2 (¼-ounce) packages active dry yeast
2½ teaspoons salt
2½ cups warm water
¾ cup oil
2 eggs, beaten

In a large bowl, combine 5 cups flour, sugar, yeast, and salt. Combine water (extra-warm, almost hot), oil, and eggs. Add to the dry ingredients and mix well. Add enough of the remaining flour to make dough easy to handle. Using only as much of the remaining flour as needed, turn dough onto lightly floured surface and knead about 10 minutes. Shape dough into a ball and place in a greased bowl, turning once to coat the top surface. Cover dough and let it rise until it doubles in size. Punch it down and let it rise again. Punch down and pinch dough into about 3 dozen balls. Place balls into well-greased pan. Let rolls rise until double in size, about 1 hour. Bake 20 to 30 minutes or until golden brown in a 375° oven.

Hushpuppies

3 cups cornmeal
1 cup all-purpose flour
¼ cup shredded Cheddar cheese
1 onion, chopped
1 teaspoon salt
1 teaspoon sugar
1 egg, beaten
⅔ cup milk
Vegetable oil for frying

Combine cornmeal, flour, cheese, onion, salt, sugar, and egg in a large bowl. Add milk (more or less as needed) to create a cookie-like dough. Roll into balls or spoon into hot grease. Cook until outside is golden brown.

Spicy Hushpuppies

3 cups cornmeal
1 cup all-purpose flour
½ cup milk
½ cup beer
½ cup shredded pepper jack cheese
1 onion, finely chopped
2 eggs, beaten

⅓ cup diced jalapeño peppers
1 teaspoon crushed red pepper
1 teaspoon sugar
1 teaspoon minced garlic
Vegetable oil for frying
Cajun seasoning for dusting

Mix all ingredients, except oil and Cajun seasoning, into a cookie-like dough. Add or reduce milk and beer as needed. Roll into balls or spoon into hot grease. Cook until outside is golden brown. Add a dusting of Cajun seasoning to hot hushpuppies as they come out of the fryer.

Cornbread Dressing

1 pan cornbread (boxed cornbread, if desired)
8 slices white bread, toasted
1 medium onion, diced
2 celery stalks, diced
2 hard-boiled eggs
3 cups chicken broth
1 tablespoon dried sage
½ teaspoon salt or to taste
1 teaspoon pepper or to taste
4 eggs, slightly beaten
½ stick butter, melted

Crumble cornbread and toasted bread in a large bowl. Add onion, celery, and eggs; mix. Add broth, sage, salt and pepper; mix. Add raw eggs and melted butter. Blend well. Pour into a buttered baking dish and bake at 425° for 20 to 30 minutes.

© Museum of Appalachia

Tennessee Fall Homecoming
Norris • Second Weekend of October for 3 days

Regional cooks prepare favorites like cornbread, fried pies, and chicken and dumplings. There are early pioneer activities such as cane grinding on a mule-powered mill, sheep herding, and lye-soap making. Festival goers enjoy performances by more than 350 traditional old-time, folk, country, gospel, and bluegrass musicians.

www.museumofappalachia.com/homecoming.htm

Tennessee

Cornbread & Ricotta Cheese Stuffing

4 cups crumbled cornbread
1¼ teaspoons salt
1 teaspoon ground black pepper
1½ teaspoons dried basil
1½ teaspoons chervil (optional)
1½ teaspoons sage
1 teaspoon dried oregano
1 cup chopped onion
½ cup freshly chopped parsley
¼ cup lightly salted butter, melted
3 eggs, lightly beaten
½ cup freshly grated Parmesan cheese
1½ cups ricotta cheese

Combine cornbread with salt, pepper, basil, chervil, sage and oregano. Toast in a warm oven spread out on a cookie sheet. Do not brown crumbs, just dry them out. In a bowl, combine cornbread mixture with onion, parsley, butter, eggs, and cheeses. Cover and chill. Use as a stuffing in chicken or turkey. Can also be baked in a greased glass baking dish at 425° until firm to the touch, about 35 to 40 minutes.

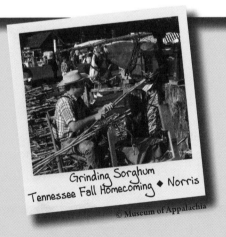

Grinding Sorghum
Tennessee Fall Homecoming ◆ Norris
© Museum of Appalachia

Coconut Cake Bread

2 cups self-rising flour
½ cup brown sugar
2 medium eggs
4 tablespoons milk
1 teaspoon lemon juice
½ teaspoon vanilla
½ cup butter, softened
½ teaspoon salt
1 cup shredded coconut, divided

Reheat slices with a big pat of melted butter–awesome.

Mix everything, except coconut, together in a bowl; mix in ⅔ cup coconut Pour into a well-greased loaf pan and bake at 325° for about 25 minutes. Top with remaining coconut, and bake an additional 5 to 10 minutes until coconut just begins to brown. Cool before slicing.

Easy Apple Butter

42 ounces unsweetened applesauce
12 ounces apple juice
2 tablespoons cinnamon
¼ teaspoon brown sugar
1 teaspoon allspice
¼ teaspoon ground cloves

Combine all ingredients in a large nonstick saucepan or crockpot. Cook 2 hours on high. Reduce heat to low and continue to cook with lid ajar to allow excess moisture to escape. Cook 2 more hours or longer. Spoon into jars or container and chill. Will darken as it cools.

Apple Bread

¾ cup sugar
¼ cup brown sugar
½ cup shortening
1 teaspoon vanilla
2 eggs, beaten
1 tablespoon buttermilk
1 tablespoon butter, melted
2 cups sifted self-rising flour
1½ cups chopped, peeled apples

TOPPING:

1 tablespoon sugar
1 tablespoon brown sugar
½ teaspoon cinnamon

For bread, cream sugars, shortening, and vanilla in a bowl with a mixer. Add eggs, buttermilk, butter, and flour mixing very well. Stir in apples. Pour into well-greased 9x13-inch glass baking dish. Spread mixture until it is smooth on top. Combine topping ingredients and sprinkle over batter. Bake 1 hour in a 325° oven or until done.

Apple Nut Bread

2 cups all-purpose flour
⅓ cup sugar
3 teaspoons baking powder
½ teaspoon salt
1 cup milk

1 egg, beaten
2 tablespoons shortening, melted
1 teaspoon vanilla
½ cup chopped nuts
2 cups diced apples

Sift dry ingredients together. Add milk, egg, melted shortening and vanilla; mix well. Stir in nuts and apples. Bake in a well-greased bread pan at 375° for 40 to 45 minutes. This recipe makes great mini loafs (use small-diced apples).

Nut Bread

¾ cup sugar

2 tablespoons shortening

1 egg, beaten

1½ cups milk

1 cup whole-wheat flour

2 cups all-purpose flour

3½ teaspoons baking powder

1 teaspoon salt

¾ cup chopped nuts

Combine all ingredients and mix well ensuring nuts are evenly distributed throughout dough. Pour into a greased and floured loaf pan. Bake at 375° for about 60 to 70 minutes. Bread should be firm in the middle.

Country Sweet Potato Bread

2 heaping cups mashed sweet potatoes

2 cups sugar

1 cup brown sugar

4 eggs, beaten

4 cups all-purpose flour

1 tablespoon baking soda

1 teaspoon salt

1 teaspoon ginger

1 teaspoon cinnamon

⅔ cup milk

Combine all ingredients in a large bowl; pour into a well-greased glass baking dish. Bake at 350° for about 45 to 60 minutes are until top springs back when pressed.

Fruit Spoonbread

2 cups milk
1 teaspoon salt
1 teaspoon brown sugar
1 cup white cornmeal
2 cups self-rising flour
2 tablespoons butter
2 eggs, beaten
1 tablespoon sugar
1 cup frozen blueberries

In a saucepan over medium heat combine milk, salt and brown sugar. When mixture simmers, spoon in cornmeal and flour until mixture thickens. Remove from heat and add butter, eggs, sugar and blueberries. Batter should be thick yet a pouring consistency—add more flour or cornmeal to thicken or add a bit more milk to thin. Pour into a well-greased bread pan or glass dish and bake at 375° for about 25 to 30 minutes. Serve hot.

World's Fair Sunsphere
Knoxville

©Wai Chan

Country White Bread

3 cups bread flour
¼ cup dry milk powder
2 tablespoons sugar
1 teaspoon salt
¼ cup butter, softened
1 egg, beaten
¼ cup water
2½ tablespoons active dry yeast

Mix all ingredients well. Knead 10 minutes. Cover and let rise until double. Punch down. Shape into a loaf. Place in greased loaf pan. Let rise until double. Bake at 350° for 30 minutes.

Bread Machine Honey Banana Whole Wheat Bread

⅔ cup warm water
1½ tablespoons butter
¼ cup honey
1 egg, beaten
½ teaspoon vanilla
1 teaspoon salt
1½ cups whole-wheat flour
1½ cups bread flour
1 banana, thinly sliced
2 teaspoons poppy seeds
2 teaspoons dry yeast

Add ingredients to pan in order listed. Cook as directed for your machine (use "Whole-Wheat" setting if available).

Sweet Beer Bread

4 cups self-rising flour
2 teaspoons sugar
1 tablespoon pancake syrup
½ teaspoon honey
2 eggs, beaten
1 can beer (dark beer is best)

Combine all ingredients. Pour into a greased bread pan and bake 55 minutes at 350°. May also cook on a covered grill using high heat.

Whole Wheat Bread

5 to 6 cups finely-ground whole-wheat flour
1 (7-gram) packet instant yeast
2 cups warm water
½ tablespoon salt
1 large egg, beaten
⅓ cup brown sugar
4 tablespoons butter, melted and slightly cooled

Place flour and yeast in a large bowl. Add warm water; mix. Add salt, egg, sugar, and butter and continue mixing for about 5 minutes. Place in large greased bowl, turning once to coat both sides; cover with plastic wrap. Refrigerate overnight or for up to three days. When ready to cook, remove dough from refrigerator and warm to room temperature (about three hours). Dough should rise to nearly double in size. Punch down and divide evenly into two loaf pans. Preheat oven to 350°. Allow loaves to double (will be very puffy). Place each pan on a shelf in the top half of the oven, well-spaced so that air can circulate between the loaves. Bake 30 minutes or until done. Remove bread from pans and cool on wire racks.

Honey Oat and Wheat Bread

2 cups milk
1 cup plus 2 tablespoons old-fashioned
 rolled oats (not instant), divided
½ cup warm water
2 (4-ounce) packages active dry yeast
½ cup honey
½ stick melted butter

3 cups whole-wheat flour
2 cups all-purpose flour
1 tablespoon salt
Vegetable oil
1 large egg, lightly beaten with
 1 tablespoon water

Heat milk in a 1½- to 2-quart saucepan over low heat until warm; stir in 1 cup oats. Remove from heat and let stand, uncovered, stirring occasionally, until cool. Add water, yeast, honey and butter; mix well. Add whole-wheat flour, all-purpose flour, salt and oat mixture, stirring until a soft dough forms. Place on a well-floured surface and knead with floured hands about 10 minutes. Form dough into a ball and transfer to an oiled large bowl. Rub top with oil, cover, and let rise until doubled in size. Punch down and break into 2 loaves. Place each in a well-greased loaf pan. Lightly brush tops of loaves with egg wash and sprinkle with 2 tablespoons oats. Bake at 375° about 30 minutes, until bread is golden. Allow to cool before cutting.

Banana Bread

¾ cup brown sugar
1 teaspoon salt
⅓ cup shortening
1 cup mashed bananas
2 eggs, beaten

2 cups all-purpose flour
1 teaspoon baking soda
½ cup milk
½ cup chopped walnuts

Combine all ingredients; mix well. Pour into a greased loaf pan. Bake at 350° 45 to 55 minutes or until done.

Sunday Brunch Monkey Bread

3 cans biscuits, cut into quarters
½ cup brown sugar
⅓ cup sugar
½ stick butter, melted
½ cup orange juice
¼ cup chopped pecans (optional)

Combine brown sugar, sugar, butter and orange juice in a large bowl. Add quartered biscuits and mix to coat all pieces. Spoon ½ biscuits into a loaf pan Sprinkle with pecans. Layer remaining biscuits on top. Bake at 350° for 30 to 35 minutes.

Hot Pepper Loaf

2 cups self-rising flour
1 cup self-rising cornmeal
2 cups milk
2 eggs, beaten
½ cup sugar
¼ cup vegetable oil
1 stick butter, softened
1 cup shredded Cheddar cheese
½ cup chopped onion
½ cup jalapeño pepper
1 teaspoon prepared horseradish
1 tablespoon minced garlic
1 teaspoon crushed red pepper

Combine all ingredients in a large bowl. Form into a well-greased well-floured bread pan. Bake at 375° for about 40 minutes, or until top is golden brown.

Cheesy Garlic-Stuffed Bread Wrap

1 canned pizza crust
½ cup butter or margarine, softened
1 teaspoon garlic powder
1 teaspoon dried parsley
⅓ cup grated Parmesan cheese
5 slices provolone cheese
Olive oil

Preheat oven to 375°. Unroll pizza crust and brush with butter. Sprinkle garlic, parsley and Parmesan evenly over crust. Spread provolone cheese evenly across top. Gently roll up as you would a sandwich wrap. Brush outside lightly with olive oil. Place on cookie sheet and cook at 350° for 15 to 20 minutes. Cover with foil if outside browns before center is cooked. You can also fold this like a calzone and add pepperoni, sausage, or other favorite toppings.

Easy Strawberry Maple Bakes

2 cans large biscuits
1 cup sliced strawberries
Chopped pecans (optional)
Cinnamon (optional)
½ stick butter
⅔ cup powdered sugar
⅓ cup maple syrup

Cut biscuits in 2 pieces. Place 1 or 2 strawberry slices in the center of half the biscuit pieces; top with a large dash of chopped pecans and cinnamon, if desired. Place remaining biscuits pieces over the top and pinch edges together. Bake as directed on biscuit can. For maple frosting, combine butter, sugar and syrup. Whip, adding more sugar or syrup if necessary to get the correct consistency. Drizzle over warm biscuits.

Salads

Seared Scallops and Spinach Salad

1 pound fresh sea scallops
2 tablespoons flour
3 teaspoons Cajun seasoning
2 tablespoons olive oil
3 cups spinach leaves
1 cup julienne carrots
1 tablespoon water
2½ tablespoons balsamic vinegar
⅓ cup sesame seeds (or sunflower seeds)
Croutons

Rinse scallops and pat dry. Combine with flour and seasoning in a zip-close bag; shake to coat. In a large skillet, heat oil and sear scallops 3 to 5 minutes or until opaque and golden. In a fresh skillet, combine spinach and carrots; sprinkle with water. Cook covered over medium-high heat until spinach starts to soften. Add vinegar and seeds; stir. Serve scallops over spinach topped with croutons. Serve hot.

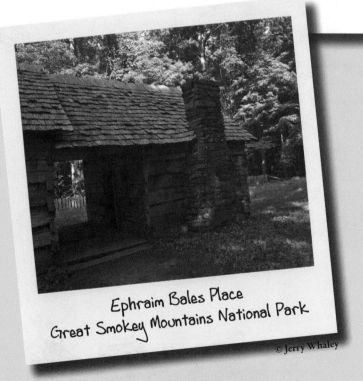

Ephraim Bales Place
Great Smokey Mountains National Park

© Jerry Whaley

Tennessee

Strawberry Salad

2 bunches spinach
4 cups sliced strawberries
½ cup vegetable oil
¼ cup white wine vinegar
½ cup sugar
¼ teaspoon paprika
2 tablespoons sesame seeds
1 tablespoon poppy seeds
Croutons or baked Chinese noodles

Rinse spinach and tear into bite-size pieces. Toss spinach and strawberries together in a large bowl. In a medium bowl, whisk together oil, vinegar, sugar, paprika, sesame seeds and poppy seeds. Pour over spinach and strawberries; toss to coat. Top with croutons or noodles before serving.

Spinach Salad

2 tablespoons cider vinegar
2 tablespoons vegetable oil
¼ teaspoon salt
¼ teaspoon sugar
¼ teaspoon black pepper
1 cup diced peeled apple
¼ cup chopped onion
¼ cup raisins
¼ cup chopped walnuts
2 cups torn fresh spinach or baby spinach leaves
2 cups torn romaine lettuce hearts
1 cup chopped carrots
Parmesan cheese

Combine vinegar, oil, salt, sugar and pepper in a small bowl; mix well. In a larger bowl, combine remaining ingredients and mix well. Stir in oil mix and gently toss. Top with a sprinkle of grated Parmesan cheese.

Strawberry, Mango & Cashew Nut Salad

1½ cups chopped strawberries
1 mango, peeled, seeded, and chopped
1 small tomato, diced
½ cup chopped cashews or other chopped nuts
½ cup freshly chopped parsley
½ cup sliced green onions
2 tablespoons fresh lime juice
1 tablespoon chopped cilantro
½ teaspoon red pepper flakes
¼ teaspoon ground cumin

Combine all ingredients and chill before serving.

A perfect side with pork and chicken. Make like a salsa and serve chilled.

©Joseph Justice • istockphoto.com

Annual Tennessee Strawberry Festival

Dayton • May

The Tennessee Strawberry Festival started in 1947 as a one-day festival to celebrate the large strawberry crops of Rhea County. At its height, Rhea County produced about four million quarts of berries each year. Now a 10-day long extravaganza, the festival is a celebration of small-town life and includes a Classic Car Cruise-in, Pancake Breakfast, Pie and Cake Baking Contest, and a Strawberry Shortcake dinner.

www.tnstrawberryfestival.com

Tennessee

Potato Salad

6 to 8 potatoes, peeled and 1-inch cubes
2 boiled eggs, chopped
½ cup sweet relish
1 small onion, diced
1 stalk celery, diced
1 teaspoon salt
1 teaspoon pepper
¼ teaspoon oregano
1 cup mayonnaise
¼ cup yellow mustard

Cook potatoes in water to cover 10 to 15 minutes, until done but still firm. Drain and rinse. Place potatoes, eggs, relish, onion and celery in a large bowl; gently toss to mix. Stir in salt, pepper, oregano, mayonnaise and mustard. Cover and chill before serving.

Dijon Potato Salad

5 small baking potatoes, cooked and diced
½ cup diced celery
¼ cup chopped onion
2 tablespoons parsley
½ tablespoon apple cider vinegar
2 tablespoons Dijon mustard
2 tablespoons yellow mustard
2 tablespoons sour cream
Salt and pepper to taste

Combine all ingredients and mix lightly. Cover and chill before serving.

Sweet and Spicy Coleslaw

1 pound cabbage, shredded
1 carrot, shredded
½ cup mayonnaise
¼ cup Dijon mustard
2 tablespoons apple vinegar
2 tablespoons sugar
1 tablespoon celery salt
Salt and pepper to taste

Combine all ingredients in a large bowl. Mix well, cover, and chill before serving.

Sweet Buttermilk Coleslaw

1 head cabbage, finely chopped
⅔ cup minced onion
1 carrot, minced
⅔ cup mayonnaise
⅓ cup buttermilk
2 tablespoons cider vinegar
2 tablespoons sugar
½ teaspoon garlic powder
1 teaspoon salt
1 teaspoon pepper

Combine ingredients in a large bowl. Mix well and cover. Chill before serving.

Asian Noodle Citrus Salad

4 cups salad greens
1 small can Mandarin oranges
1 cup sour cream
1 teaspoon lemon juice
1 teaspoon brown sugar
1 cup baked Chinese noodles
½ cup chopped almonds
Salt and pepper

Rinse, pat dry and toss greens. Drain juice from oranges into a small bowl. Set oranges aside. Add sour cream, lemon juice and brown sugar to juice to make a dressing. Stir to mix well. Add oranges to greens, pour on dressing, and toss to coat. Serve in bowls topped with noodles, almonds and a dash of salt and pepper.

Crispy Slaw Chefs Salad

1 bag prepared mixed salad greens
1 bag finely-sliced or angel hair slaw mix
1 cup chopped ham
1 cup chopped turkey
½ cup bacon bits
2 hard-boiled eggs, sliced
2 tablespoons Italian seasoning
Favorite dressing

Mix salad greens and slaw mix together in a large bowl. Top with ham, turkey, bacon bits, eggs and Italian seasoning. Serve in large bowl with your favorite dressing.

Edamame Mixed Salad

1 small bag mixed salad greens
1 bag frozen shelled edamame, thawed and dried
   (green soybeans)
1 cucumber, sliced
½ cup chopped radishes
½ cup chopped carrots
¼ cup seasoned rice vinegar
1 tablespoon vegetable oil
2 tablespoons flavored yogurt
¼ teaspoon salt
½ teaspoon black pepper

Combine greens, edamame, cucumber, radishes and carrots in a large bowl. Mix by hand. In a small bowl combine remaining ingredients; stir into salad greens. Chill before serving.

Tennessee Soybean Festival
Martin • September

The Tennessee Soybean Festival celebrates the benefits of soybeans and the community of Martin, home of the University of Tennessee, with a wide range of activities. Held for four days in September, the festival features a soybean pancake tournament, golf tournament, street fair, bicycle rodeo, car show, senior citizens shuffleboard tournament, mini quilt show, barbecue, kids' day, and high school rodeo challenge.

www.tnsoybeanfestival.org

©Tennessee Soybean Festival

Tennessee

Smoked Pork Salad

4 cups mixed salad greens
½ pound pulled barbecue pork, without sauce
1 cup cornbread crumbs
1 cup shredded cheese
Favorite dressing

Divide greens onto plates; top with pork, cornbread crumbs and shredded cheese. Add other favorite ingredients, as desired. Serve with favorite dressing.

Tossed Greens & Turkey Salad

1 bag mixed salad greens
1 cup broccoli pieces
1 cup cauliflower pieces
2 cups chopped turkey or chicken (use pre-cooked or
 left-over meat that has been chilled)
½ cup bacon bits
½ cup seasoned croutons
1 cup Italian dressing

Combine all ingredients in a bowl, cover and toss. Chill at lease 5 minutes before serving.

Chicken Salad

4 cooked chicken breasts,
  cubed
¼ teaspoon minced garlic
Olive oil
1 medium onion, diced
4 stalks celery, diced
¼ cup Dijon mustard
⅔ cup mayonnaise
1 tablespoon basil
1 tablespoon garlic
1 tablespoon black pepper
⅓ cup chopped almonds

Gently sauté chicken with garlic in olive oil until edges are brown. Mix with remaining ingredients; place in a covered bowl. Chill for a few hours before serving.

Pasta Salad

16 ounces rotini pasta
8 ounces pepperoni
1 tablespoon plus 1 teaspoon
  Durkee salad seasoning
1½ cups ranch dressing

Cook pasta to al dente. Drain and rinse with cold water until pasta is cool. Drain well. Add remaining ingredients. Serve chilled.

Tossed Okra Salad

1 (16-ounce) package breaded okra
1 large tomato, chopped
⅔ cup cauliflower pieces
½ small onion, chopped
12 slices bacon, cooked and crumbled

Fry okra in hot oil and drain on paper towel. Place okra and remaining ingredients in a large bowl. Toss and serve.

Mixed Vegetable Salad with Creamy Dressing

Mixed Vegetable Salad:

2 cups broccoli pieces
2 cups cauliflower pieces
½ cup diced red onion
1½ cups chopped carrots
½ cup shredded cabbage (optional)
1 cup shredded Swiss or Monterey Jack cheese
½ cup bacon bits
½ teaspoon salt
½ teaspoon pepper
½ cup chopped almonds or walnuts

Creamy Dressing:

1 cup mayonnaise
1 cup sour cream
1 tablespoon lemon juice
1 tablespoon sugar

In a large bowl, combine salad ingredients. Toss to mix. In a small bowl, combine dressing ingredients. Pour over salad and toss gently. Chill before serving.

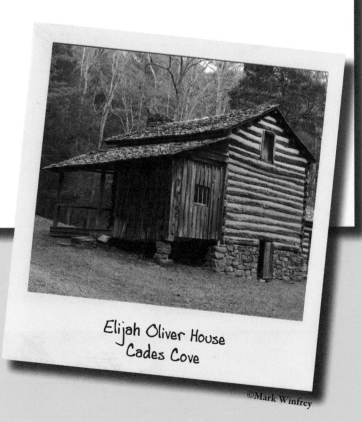

Elijah Oliver House
Cades Cove

©Mark Winfrey

Italian Tomato Salad

1 bottle Italian dressing
2 large cucumbers, peeled and thinly sliced
2 to 3 tomatoes, sliced
1 medium onion, sliced
Parsley for garnish

In a large bowl combine all ingredients except parsley. Toss and chill. When ready to serve, garnish with parsley and serve cold.

Cauliflower Salad

4 to 5 cups cauliflower pieces
3 celery stalks, chopped
2 onions, chopped
3 hard-boiled eggs, peeled and chopped
3 tablespoons mayonnaise
2 tablespoons yellow mustard
1 tablespoon apple cider vinegar
Salt and pepper
Cajun seasoning

Cook cauliflower using desired method; drain and cool. Combine cooled cauliflower with remaining ingredients. Mix well, cover and chill. Serve like potato salad.

Soups, Stews, Chilis & Chowders

Black Bean Soup

¾ pound black beans
1½ quarts cold water
¾ pound ham hock or
   bone of smoke ham
1 large onion, diced
2 green bell peppers, diced
1 can whole-kernel corn, drained

1 tablespoon minced garlic
½ cup olive oil
1 bay leaf
1 tablespoon seasoned salt
⅛ teaspoon oregano
¼ teaspoon Worcestershire sauce
¼ cup vinegar

Sort beans to remove stones, etc. Wash beans then soak in cool water overnight. Rinse beans. Transfer to a stock pot; add water to cover beans by two inches. Add remaining ingredients, except vinegar, and simmer until beans are tender and thick, approximately 3 hours. Add additional water for soup consistency. Add vinegar about 10 minutes before serving. Great with rice, cornbread and chopped onion.

Ally's Tex Mex Soup

1 pound hamburger, browned and drained
1 large can stewed tomatoes
1 large can tomato sauce
1 can whole-kernel corn
1 large can kidney beans
1 small sweet onion, diced
1 package taco seasoning
1 small can diced green chilies
½ tablespoon cumin powder
Salt and pepper to taste
Grated cheese, sour cream, and corn chips for garnish

Put all ingredients, except those for garnish, in crockpot; stir well. Cook on high 4 hours. Serve with grated cheese, sour cream, and corn chips.

Smoked Sausage and Lentil Soup

1 pound smoked sausage, sliced
1 pound lentils
1 small onion, chopped
1 stalk celery, sliced
2 carrots, sliced
½ teaspoon minced garlic
2 teaspoons salt
1½ teaspoons oregano
1 can tomato paste
8 cups water
1 can diced tomatoes

In a large pot combine all ingredients, except 1 can diced tomatoes. Bring to a boil; cover and simmer 1 hour. When lentils are tender, add tomatoes and simmer an additional 20 minutes. Serve hot.

Can a Can Beef Soup

1 pound ground beef
1 small onion, chopped
1 can mixed vegetables
1 can cream corn
1 can diced tomatoes
1 can green chilies
1 can Spanish rice
1 tablespoon steak sauce
Salt and pepper to taste

In a large stock pot, brown and drain the ground beef. Add remaining ingredients, cover, and simmer about 1 hour. Substitute chopped stew meat for ground beef, if desired.

Crockpot Harvest Soup

1 pound ground beef
3 cups water
1 small onion, chopped
2 stalks celery, finely chopped
2 carrots, finely chopped
2 cups diced potatoes
2 cans stewed tomatoes
1 can tomato paste
2 cups shredded cabbage
1 envelope onion soup mix
Salt and pepper to taste

Brown and drain meat. Combine with remaining ingredients in a large crockpot; cook on high 3 to 4 hours. Add other ½ pack onion soup mix and additional water, if desired.

Italian Sausage Soup

2 pounds Italian sausage
2 cups sliced celery
1 large can tomato sauce
2 cans diced tomatoes
1 teaspoon minced garlic
2 green bell peppers, diced
1 large onion, diced
1 large zucchini, peeled and diced
1 tablespoon grated Parmesan cheese
1 teaspoon Italian seasoning
½ teaspoon crushed oregano
½ teaspoon sugar

Slice or break up sausage and brown in skillet. In a large pot, combine sausage with remaining ingredients; cook about 2 hours. Serve with toasted garlic bread.

Easy Minestrone Soup

1 pound fresh spinach
½ cup crushed **Ritz** crackers
1½ pounds lean ground beef
1 egg
Salt and pepper to taste
3 tablespoons olive oil
1 can diced tomatoes
1 large can kidney beans
1 large onion, finely chopped

1 cup chopped celery
1 cup sliced carrots
½ tablespoon oregano
½ teaspoon basil
½ cup uncooked elbow macaroni
4 cups water
3 beef bouillon cubes
Parmesan cheese

Wash, dry and finely chop spinach. In a bowl combine spinach, cracker crumbs, beef, egg, salt and pepper. Shape into small meatballs. In a skillet, brown meatballs on all sides; remove from heat. In a stockpot, combine remaining ingredients and simmer until noodles are almost done. Stir in meatballs. Add additional seasonings, as desired. Continue to cook until meatballs are warm and noodles are done. Serve hot.

Riverfront
Chattanooga

©Jeff Kinsey

Rich and Creamy Tomato Soup

2 cans peeled tomatoes, undrained
2 tablespoons butter
1 large onion, chopped
1 carrot, chopped
1 tablespoon minced garlic
3 cups water
2 chicken bouillon cubes
1 small potato, diced
2 teaspoons basil
¼ teaspoon nutmeg
½ teaspoon salt
½ teaspoon black pepper
1 cup milk

Using a blender, pureé tomatoes with liquid. Add remaining ingredients, processing frequently to mince ingredients. Pour pureé into a pot and simmer on medium for about 1 hour. Reduce heat and blend small batches of soup until creamy. Return soup to pot and simmer a few more minutes before serving.

Grainger County Tomato Festival
Rutledge • Last weekend in July

The Grainger County Tomato Festival was organized in 1993 to promote the local tomato crops and to provide exposure for area artists, craftsman and non-profit organizations. Events include music, beauty pageant, 5k run, art show, car show, Civil War camp, and tomato wars. This event is sponsored by the Rutledge Lion's Club and has become one of the largest free festivals in East Tennessee.

www.graingercountytomatofestival.com

©Grainger County Tomato Festival

Tennessee

Zucchini Soup

3 cups water
1 chicken bouillon cube
½ beef bouillon cube
3 medium zucchini, sliced
1 small bell pepper, diced
1 small onion, diced

1 teaspoon dill
1 teaspoon black pepper
½ teaspoon salt
1 cup sour cream
Paprika
Parsley

In a large saucepan, combine water, bouillon cubes, zucchini, bell pepper and onion. Cover and simmer 20 minutes or until veggies are tender. Add dill, pepper, and salt. Reduce heat and cool slightly. Pour into a food processor or blender and pureé. Return to saucepan and reheat. Stir in sour cream and blend well. Serve in a bowl topped with paprika and parsley.

Chicken Stock Vegetable Soup

6 cups water
2 chicken bouillon cubes
1 can tomato sauce
4 medium potatoes, diced
2 carrots, chopped
1½ onions, chopped
¼ cup chopped celery
¼ cup chopped bell pepper

1 handful uncooked rice
1 teaspoon basil
½ teaspoon parsley
½ teaspoon dill
½ teaspoon pepper
1 teaspoon Worcestershire sauce
1½ teaspoons salt

Combine all ingredients in a stock pot and simmer until potatoes are tender. Add additional water as needed.

Potato Soup

3 potatoes, peeled
2 cups milk
½ small onion, minced
3 tablespoons butter
2 tablespoons all-purpose flour
1 teaspoon salt
1 teaspoon black pepper
½ teaspoon cumin
½ teaspoon celery salt
¼ teaspoon cayenne pepper
1 teaspoon chopped parsley

Cook potatoes in salted water, drain and mash with a fork. In a pot, over medium heat, add 1 cup water, 2 cups milk and diced onion. Bring to a simmer then stir in potatoes and remaining ingredients. Simmer to desired thickness stirring often. Milk can be added to thin; flour can be added to thicken. Serve hot.

Ramp & Potato Soup

6 medium potatoes, peeled
  and diced
1 small red onion, chopped
3 cups water
2 cups chopped cooked ham
2 teaspoons salt

½ teaspoon pepper
2 cups milk
2 cups cleaned chopped ramps
3 tablespoons flour
Paprika for garnish

In a stockpot, combine potatoes, onion and 3 cups water. Bring to a boil and add remaining ingredients except ramps and flour. Cook until potatoes are tender. Stir in ramps; add flour, if needed, to thicken. Add milk, if needed to thin. Cook until ramps are tender. Top with paprika when serving.

Broccoli & Cheese Soup

1 cup water
1 chicken bouillon cube
1 small package frozen broccoli
1 medium carrot, finely chopped
1 small onion, finely chopped
1 celery stalk, finely chopped
2 tablespoons butter
3 tablespoons all-purpose flour
2 cups milk
1 pound processed cheese, cubed
1 can cream of chicken soup
1 tablespoon Worcestershire sauce
Salt and pepper to taste

Combine all ingredients in a stockpot or large saucepan and cook over medium to low heat until cheese melts. Simmer, adding milk as needed, about 20 minutes. Serve with tortilla chips, crackers or pita bread.

Vegetable Cheese Soup

2 cups chopped carrots
2 cups chopped celery
2 cups cauliflower pieces
1 large onion, diced
1 green bell pepper, diced
4 tablespoons butter
2 tablespoons flour
1 cup milk
1 can evaporated milk
1 can chicken broth
Salt and pepper to taste
1 pound processed cheese, cubed

Combine all ingredients, except cheese, in a large pot. Cook, covered, over medium heat until veges are tender. Slowly add cubed cheese and stir until melted. Serve hot.

Cool Tomato Gazpacho

3 medium tomatoes, seeds removed and finely diced
1 large bell pepper, seeds removed and finely diced
1 cucumber, seeds removed and finely diced
1 sweet onion, diced
1 teaspoon minced garlic
½ teaspoon salt
1 teaspoon chives
1 teaspoon parsley
1 teaspoon basil
1 teaspoon tarragon
½ cup olive oil
1 tablespoon lemon juice
3 cups water
1 teaspoon paprika
Black pepper
Crushed croutons for garnish

In a large bowl, combine all ingredients except black pepper and croutons. Leave as-is for a chunky gazpacho or blend in blender to a smooth consistency. Chill and serve cold topped with black pepper and crushed croutons.

Tomato Art Fest
Greater Five Points of Nashville
August

Tomatoes abound at this festival featuring the artwork of over 100 skilled artists from around the country, an heirloom tomato tasting, Tomatillo! Children's Fine Art, a "Most Beautiful Tomato" competition, a Bloody Mary contest, and a tomato recipe contest with six categories—including dessert!

www.tomatoartfest.com

©Aerial Innovations of Tennessee, Inc. www.flytenn.com

Tennessee

Beef Stew

2 pounds stew meat
Oil
Black pepper
2 cups water
⅓ cup brewed coffee
1½ cups diced celery
4 to 6 carrots, diced
3 medium potatoes, diced
1 to 2 large onions, diced
1 large can stewed tomatoes
1 cup small-cut mushrooms
1 can whole-kernel corn
1 tablespoon salt
1 tablespoon black pepper
1 tablespoon yellow mustard
Garlic powder to taste
½ tablespoon basil
½ teaspoon thyme
2 tablespoons sugar
2 teaspoons Worcestershire sauce

Brown stew meat in a small amount of oil; sprinkle with black pepper. Combine remaining ingredients in a stockpot and bring to a simmer. Stir in stew meat, cover and simmer about 2 hours. If necessary, add water to thin or flour to thicken.

Brunswick Stew

½ cup butter or margarine
3 cups cooked chopped chicken
3 cups chopped potatoes
2 cups chopped smoked pork
1 cup diced onion
½ cup diced green bell pepper
2 cups water
1 beef bouillon cube

1 chicken bouillon cube
2 cans stewed tomatoes
1 can chili beans
1 can cream-style corn
1 can green peas
¼ cup liquid smoke
1½ cups barbecue sauce

Combine all ingredients in a large pot or crockpot. Cook on medium (high if using crockpot) about 2 hours. Serve topped with crumbled cornbread and shredded cheese.

Crockpot Brunswick Stew

1 medium onion, chopped
1 small green bell pepper, chopped
2 (16-ounce) cans crushed tomatoes
1 pound shredded barbecued pork
2 cans whole-kernel corn
1 can cream-style corn
½ cup barbecue sauce
½ teaspoon salt
1½ teaspoons pepper
1 tablespoon sugar

Combine all ingredients in crockpot. Cook on low 5 to 6 hours, covered.

Chicken Stew

4 to 5 chicken breasts, cooked and cubed
Olive oil
2 cans mixed vegetables
1 can cream of mushroom soup
1 can diced tomatoes
1½ cups water
½ cup sour cream
1 small green bell pepper, diced
½ tablespoon garlic salt
½ tablespoon black pepper
½ tablespoon oregano
1 teaspoon basil

Fry cooked chicken in a skillet with olive oil to golden color. Combine with remaining ingredients in a large saucepan, cover and simmer about an hour. Add milk to thin, if needed. Thin more for a soup or allow to thicken and use as a chicken pot pie recipe using pie shells for crust.

Oyster Stew

1 pint jar oysters
⅓ cup finely diced celery
¼ cup butter
¾ teaspoon salt
½ teaspoon pepper
¼ teaspoon paprika plus more for garnish
1 quart milk
Parsley

In a large saucepan, combine oysters, celery and butter. Cook for about 5 minutes. Add salt, pepper, paprika and milk; simmer 10 minutes. Serve hot topped with paprika and parsley and crackers on the side.

Beef Stew Chili

2 pounds beef for stew, ½-inch
  pieces
2 tablespoons vegetable oil
½ teaspoon salt
½ teaspoon pepper
½ teaspoon chili powder
1 cup ready-to-serve beef broth
1 jar prepared thick-and-chunky
  salsa
2 medium zucchini, diced
1 can black beans, rinsed, drained
1 can whole-kernel corn
1 can diced tomatoes
1 medium onion, diced
1 green bell pepper, diced
1 pack chili mix
1 tablespoon cumin powder
Hot sauce to taste

In a skillet, brown meat with oil, salt, pepper and chili powder. When brown, combine in stockpot with remaining ingredients. Cover and simmer 1 hour.

Dark Beer Crockpot Chili

1 pound ground beef
1 pound hot ground sausage
1 can dark beer
½ cup diced onion
½ cup diced green bell pepper
2 cans kidney beans
1 can tomatoes
1 can tomato paste
1 tablespoon minced garlic
2 tablespoons chili powder
1 tablespoon soy sauce
Salt and pepper to taste

Brown meat; drain. Break into small pieces and combine with remaining ingredients in a large crockpot. Cook on low 6 hours or high 3 hours.

Easy Crockpot Chili

1 pound ground beef, browned
1 cup chopped green bell pepper
1 cup chopped onion
3 tablespoons chili powder
2 cloves garlic, minced
2 cans condensed tomato soup
2 cans kidney beans
1 tablespoon white vinegar
1 teaspoon cinnamon

In a large crockpot, combine all ingredients and cook on high 3 hours or more.

Meaty Chili

2½ pounds ground beef
1 pound ground sausage
1 pound thin-sliced smoked sausage
Vegetable oil
1½ cups coarsely chopped onion
1½ cups chopped green bell pepper
1 tablespoon minced garlic
1 tablespoon black pepper
1 teaspoon salt

2 cans diced tomatoes
2 cans chili beans
1 can black beans
1 can tomato paste
3 tablespoons chili powder
1 teaspoon dried oregano leaves
½ teaspoon crushed red pepper
2 tablespoons steak sauce

Brown meats in oil crumbling into small pieces. Combine with remaining ingredients in a stockpot and simmer 2 to 3 hours.

Cream Corn Chowder

1 can whole-kernel corn
2 cans cream-style corn
3 cups water
1 chicken bouillon cube
4 potatoes, peeled and diced
1 medium onion, diced
2 stalks celery, diced
¼ teaspoon pepper
⅓ cup milk
½ cup American cheese

In a stockpot, combine corn, water, and bouillon cube. Bring to a boil then allow to boil 3 minutes. Add potatoes, onion, celery, and pepper. Cook until potatoes are falling apart; stir in milk and cheese. Add milk to thin or flour to thicken if needed. Serve hot.

Clam Chowder

2 cans minced clams
2½ cups finely chopped
    potatoes
1 cup finely chopped onions
1 cup finely chopped celery
1 cup finely grated carrots
¾ cup butter
1½ teaspoons sugar
½ teaspoon black pepper
1½ teaspoons salt
1 tablespoon parsley
¾ cup flour
1 pint whipping cream
1 pint milk

In a saucepan, drain liquid from clams (reserve clams); add vegetables and water to barely cover. Simmer until tender. Put clams in a small skillet with butter and cook until very slightly browned. Stir in remaining ingredients and cook until thick. Add to veggies and cook on medium-low for about an hour. Serve hot topped with oyster crackers and paprika.

Vegetables &
Other Side Dishes

Country-Fried Okra

1 pound small okra pods
¾ cup cornmeal
¼ cup flour
Salt and pepper
Oil

Wash okra and cut off ends of pods; cut into ½-inch slices. Moisten slightly and shake in paper bag containing cornmeal, flour, salt, and pepper. Fry in hot oil until golden brown. Serve hot.

Roasted Cheddar Potatoes

4 to 6 potatoes, wedge-cut with skin
Nonstick spray
1 teaspoon paprika
1 teaspoon chili powder
1 teaspoon parsley
½ teaspoon salt
1 teaspoon garlic powder
1 cup shredded white or sharp Cheddar cheese
⅔ cup crushed croutons

Place potatoes in a large zip-close plastic bag. Spray nonstick spray into bag to evenly coat potatoes. In a small bowl, combine paprika, chili powder, parsley, salt, and garlic powder. Pour into bag and shake to coat potatoes. On a cookie sheet with nonstick spray, spread the potatoes in a single layer. Sprinkle on additional coating mix, if desired. Bake at 350° for 40 minutes, until potatoes begin to get tender and brown. In another small bowl, combine cheese and croutons. Sprinkle over potatoes just before removing from oven and continue to cook just until cheese is melted.

Ranch Potato Slices

4 large baking potatoes
Butter
1 medium onion, sliced
2 cloves garlic, minced
1 tablespoon red pepper (or to taste)
1 tablespoon freshly chopped thyme
Salt and pepper to taste
1 packet ranch dressing mix, divided
1 cup sour cream
½ teaspoon orange juice

Scrub potatoes, and slice ¼-inch thick. Place on large cookie sheet or roasting pan. Apply a dot of butter to each potato piece. Spread sliced onions throughout potatoes. Sprinkle potatoes and onions with garlic, red pepper, thyme, salt and pepper, and ½ ranch dressing mix. Bake at 375° for 45 minutes or until potatoes are soft. In a small bowl, stir remaining ranch mix with sour cream and orange juice. Mix, chill, and serve with hot potatoes.

Easy Potato Supreme

10 to 12 potatoes, peeled
Salt and pepper
1½ pints whipping cream
Paprika
Parsley

Finely shred potatoes and place in a large glass baking dish. Stir in salt and pepper to taste. Pour whipping cream over potatoes and bake at 350° 1½ hours. Top with paprika and parsley before serving. Serve hot.

Scalloped Potatoes

6 medium potatoes, sliced
1½ cups shredded cheese
⅓ cup chopped onion
1 cup sour cream
1 can cream of chicken soup
¼ cup butter, melted
½ cup milk
Pepper

Cook potatoes in salted water until barely tender. In a large bowl, combine potatoes and remaining ingredients; place in oven-safe dish coated with oil or nonstick spray. Cook at 375° for 35 to 40 minutes, or until tops of potatoes begin to brown. Serve hot.

Baked-Flavored Mashed Potatoes

4 large potatoes, peeled and cubed
¾ cup sour cream
½ cup nonfat milk
2 tablespoons Dijon mustard
⅓ cup minced onion
½ tablespoon minced garlic
Salt and ground black pepper to taste

Place cubed potatoes in a pot with enough water to cover. Bring to a boil and cook 15 minutes, or until tender. Drain potatoes and transfer to a bowl. Mash and gradually mix in sour cream, nonfat milk, and Dijon mustard. Season with onion, garlic, salt and pepper.

Scalloped Potatoes & Ham

3 pounds potatoes, peeled and sliced
1 cup shredded Cheddar cheese
½ cup chopped onion
¼ cup minced green bell pepper
1 cup cooked cubed ham
½ cup cooked bacon
1 can cream of mushroom soup
½ cup water
½ teaspoon garlic powder
¼ teaspoon salt
¼ teaspoon black pepper

Place sliced potatoes in slow cooker. Combine remaining ingredients; add to slow cooker. Cover and cook on high for 4 hours.

The Hermitage, Home of President Andrew Jackson Nashville

©aceshot1

Candied Yams

¼ cup butter
½ cup brown sugar
1 (15-ounce) can Bruce's Louisiana Yams

Melt butter in skillet and stir in brown sugar. Add yams and turn to coat with syrup mixture. Cook over medium heat until glazed, about 15 minutes, turning and basting occasionally.

Fried Sweet Taters

3 to 4 large sweet potatoes
Oil for deep frying
Salt and pepper
Garlic powder
1 tablespoon cinnamon
1 tablespoon sugar

Cut sweet potatoes into thick French fry strips. Put strips in ice water until ready to fry. Dry with paper towels and fry, in batches, in hot oil until lightly browned. Drain on paper towels. While still hot, coat with dashes of salt, pepper, and garlic powder. Combine cinnamon and brown sugar in a shallow dish and toss fries before serving.

Ketner's Mill Country Arts Fair
Lookout Mountain
Third weekend in October

This festival is situated at a beautiful historic mill and dam on the Sequatchie River. Built in 1882, by 'Pappy' A.K. Ketner, the site includes a grist mill, sawmill, and large working water wheel. The festival is on 100 acres next to the Mill and is set among historic farm buildings. The small pavilion next to the Mill houses some displays of art, crafts, and domestic arts displays such as wool spinning and weaving, sorghum grinding, chair caning, and country cooking with the Mill's freshly ground cornmeal. Stoneground cornmeal and grits are for sale. Music performance includes the area's best bluegrass, country, and gospel groups.

www.ketnersmill.org

Roasted Rosemary Sweet Potatoes

2 pounds sweet potatoes, peeled, 1½ inch-pieces
3 large garlic cloves, coarsely chopped
1 tablespoon freshly chopped rosemary
2 tablespoons olive oil
½ cup toasted pine nuts
2 tablespoons chopped parsley
1 teaspoon salt
¼ teaspoon ground pepper

In roasting pan, combine sweet potatoes, garlic, rosemary and oil. Toss to blend well. Roast at 375° for 50 minutes, or until tender, turning occasionally. Just before serving, season with pine nuts, parsley, salt and pepper.

Baked Honey Sweet Potato Wedges

3 to 4 sweet potatoes
1 stick butter
1 tablespoon honey
1 teaspoon brown sugar

Slice potatoes into 4 equal wedges. Coat wedges with butter and bake at 350° about 40 minutes, until tender. Before removing from oven brush with honey and a light coating of brown sugar.

Cucumbers

4 medium cucumbers,
  thinly sliced
½ cup vinegar
¼ cup cold water
2 tablespoons chopped dill
3 tablespoons sugar
½ teaspoon salt
Dash pepper

Combine sliced cucumber with all other ingredients; cover and chill.

Brown Rice and Apricot Pilaf

¾ cup uncooked brown rice
3 cups chicken broth
½ cup regular barley
¼ cup apricots
¼ cup dried currants
1 tablespoon butter
⅓ cup sliced almonds

In a medium saucepan combine rice and chicken broth and bring to boil. After a 2-minute boil, reduce heat to medium low and cover. Simmer 15 to 20 minutes; remove from heat. Stir in barley, apricots, currants, and butter. Spoon the mixture into a casserole dish, cover and bake at 325° for 45 minutes or until rice and barley are tender and liquid is absorbed. Just before serving, fluff rice mixture with a fork and mix in almonds.

Tennessee

Fried Green Tomatoes & Onions with Honey Dijon Sauce

Honey Dijon Sauce:

3 tablespoons sour cream or plain yogurt
2 tablespoons Dijon mustard
1 tablespoon honey
1 tablespoon water

Combine sauce ingredients in a small bowl, mix, chill and serve.

Fried Green Tomatoes & Onions:

3 green tomatoes
3 red tomatoes
1 large onion, thickly sliced
2 eggs
½ cup milk
½ cup cornmeal
½ cup flour
Salt and pepper
Garlic salt (optional)
Oil for frying

Slice tomatoes and onions into thick slices. Combine eggs and milk; beat well. Combine cornmeal, flour, salt, pepper and garlic salt; mix well. Dip each piece of tomato and onion in egg mixture then cornmeal mix. Fry in hot oil until golden brown. Layer a slice of fried red tomato, topped with a fried onion, topped with a slice of fried green tomato. Garnish with parsley and a side of cornbread. Serve with Honey Dijon Sauce drizzled over the top.

Green Beans and Onions

2 cans green beans
  or equal amount freshly snapped beans
½ small onion, sliced
1 beef bouillon cube
½ tablespoon milk
Salt
Garlic powder

In a saucepan, combine beans, onions, bouillon cube and milk. Add water to top of beans. Cover and simmer 20 minutes. Before serving, add a dash of salt and garlic powder.

Vegetable Combo Dish

2 cups chopped onion
2 cups freshly chopped tomato
2 cups chopped zucchini
2 cups chopped bell pepper
1 envelope favorite dry soup mix
½ teaspoon salt
½ teaspoon pepper

Place onion, tomato, zucchini and pepper in bowl; add dry soup mix, salt and pepper. Toss lightly until ingredients are combined; place into a non-stick glass baking dish. Bake uncovered at 350° for 45 minutes. Serve hot.

Green Beans and Ham

1½ cups cooked ham, diced
3 cans French-style green beans, drained
1 medium onion, chopped
½ cup chopped mushrooms
½ cup butter
½ cup sesame seeds
1 teaspoon salt

In a large saucepan, cook ham and beans in water to cover over medium heat until heated through. Sauté onions and mushrooms in a small skillet with butter. Stir in sesame seeds until browned. Drain beans; combine with salt and sautéed mixture in serving bowl. Serve hot.

Veggie Melody with Buttered Pecans

1 can green beans, drained
1 can peas, drained
1 can carrots, drained
1 chicken bouillon cube
½ teaspoon celery salt
½ teaspoon pepper
2 tablespoons butter
4 tablespoons chopped pecans
¼ teaspoon pepper
Parmesan cheese

Cook vegetables in a saucepan with bouillon, celery salt, pepper, and water to cover. Boil and reduce heat to a simmer for 15 minutes. Melt butter in nonstick skillet; add pecans and cook until golden, stirring often. Drain vegetables and add to skillet; mix and cook until thoroughly heated. Sprinkle with pepper and Parmesan cheese. Serve hot.

Garden Fresh Vegetables & Rice

2½ cups freshly sliced mushrooms

1 onion, chopped

1 tablespoon minced garlic

2 tablespoons olive oil

1 cup uncooked rice

3 cups vegetable or chicken broth, divided

¼ cup bite-size broccoli pieces

¼ cup shredded carrot

½ cup seeded and chopped tomato

1 cup shredded Muenster cheese

¼ cup Parmesan cheese

2 tablespoons basil

1 teaspoon salt

1½ teaspoons cracked black pepper

In a large saucepan, cook mushrooms, onion, and garlic in oil until onion is tender. Stir in uncooked rice. Cook until rice is golden. Add additional oil as needed. Add ½ of the broth and all the broccoli; stir. Continue to cook and stir until liquid is absorbed and rice begins to soften. Add remaining broth, carrots, tomatoes, cheeses and basil. Cook and stir until creamy. Add salt and pepper, stir and serve hot. Top with additional Parmesan cheese, if desired.

Covered Bridge
Harrisburg

©Jerry Whaley

Garden Vegetable Gratin

2 small zucchini, chopped
2 small yellow summer squash, chopped
2 large leeks, chopped
1 bell pepper, chopped
1 small onion, sliced
2 tablespoons olive oil, divided
Salt and pepper
2 tablespoons fine dry breadcrumbs
2 tablespoons finely shredded Parmesan cheese
2 teaspoons freshly snipped thyme
½ tablespoon minced garlic

In a baking dish coated with nonstick cooking spray, combine zucchini, squash, leeks, bell pepper, onion, and 1 tablespoon olive oil. Evenly coat with dashes of salt and black pepper. In a small bowl, combine 1 tablespoon olive oil, breadcrumbs, Parmesan cheese, thyme, and garlic. Sprinkle over vegetables. Bake in a 425° oven for 20 to 25 minutes.

Carrots au Gratin

1 pound carrots, sliced
¼ cup dry breadcrumbs
1 tablespoon butter, melted
1 can cream of celery soup
1 cup shredded Cheddar
  cheese
1 tablespoon parsley
1 teaspoon rosemary

In a medium saucepan, cook carrots in a small amount of water until tender; drain. In a small bowl, combine breadcrumbs and melted butter. In a medium bowl, combine cooked carrots, soup, cheese, parsley, and rosemary. Pour into baking dish and sprinkle with breadcrumb mixture. Bake at 350° for 25 minutes.

Stir-Fried Sugar Snap Peas and Baby Carrots

20 baby carrots, sliced in half lengthwise
½ pound sugar snap peas, stringed
1½ teaspoons vegetable oil
3 tablespoons water
1 teaspoon chicken bouillon powder
1 tablespoon minced garlic
Salt and pepper

Cook carrots in large pot of boiling salted water until almost crisp, about 4 minutes. Add peas and cook until vegetables are crisp-tender. Drain and dry vegetables. In a large nonstick skillet, stir-fry vegetables in oil over high heat for 1 minute. Combine 3 tablespoons water and chicken bouillon powder. Add to vegetables in skillet; stir-fry 1 minute. Add garlic; stir-fry until edges begin to brown. Season with salt and pepper, as desired.

Bacon-Boiled Spinach

1½ pounds spinach, trimmed, rinsed
  and patted dry
½ teaspoon salt
2 tablespoons butter
1 piece uncooked bacon

Place all ingredients in a large pot of boiling water. Cover and boil 5 to 8 minutes. Remove bacon and serve hot.

Skillet Mushrooms

1 pound large fresh button mushrooms
Olive oil
1 teaspoon Dijon mustard
½ cup cooked and crumbled bacon
Parsley

Heat oil in skillet. Add mushrooms and cook, stirring constantly, 1 to 2 minutes or just until mushrooms start to brown. Stir in mustard and cook until mushrooms are tender. Sprinkle with bacon and parsley; serve hot.

Mushrooms Supreme

½ cup minced onion
4 tablespoons butter, divided
1½ pounds mushrooms, sliced
1½ tablespoons all-purpose flour
2 cups sour cream
⅓ cup freshly chopped parsley

Topping:
1½ tablespoons butter or margarine
3 tablespoons dry or fresh breadcrumbs
3 tablespoons freshly chopped parsley

In a large skillet, sauté onion in 3 tablespoons butter until soft and golden. Stir in mushrooms and cook over medium-high heat until tender. Add 1 tablespoon butter if needed and stir in flour, sour cream and parsley. Stir well and pour into a baking dish. Bake at 325° about 20 minutes. Combine topping ingredients and sprinkle over top; cook an additional 5 minutes or until topping has browned.

Baked Asparagus with Parmesan Cheese

2 pounds asparagus
4 tablespoons butter
1 cup freshly grated Parmesan cheese

Preheat oven to 400°. Trim asparagus and boil in lightly salted water 2 to 3 minutes. Do not overcook; asparagus should be firm and not limp. Drain asparagus and place lengthwise in a buttered baking dish. Top with remaining butter and bake until top forms a light brown crust. Cover with cheese and serve hot.

Bacon-Topped Brussels Sprouts

1 pound bacon
1 small onion, diced
2 pounds Brussels sprouts, trimmed and halved
Salt and pepper
Dash of basil
Dash of thyme
1 cup chicken broth

Fry bacon in skillet until done; crumble and set aside. Sauté onions in bacon grease 1 to 2 minutes. Add Brussels sprouts and brown edges slightly. Season with salt, pepper, basil and thyme. Add broth, cover, and simmer about 10 minutes. Before serving, top with reserved bacon.

Fried Collard Greens

1 pound frozen collards
4 tablespoons butter or bacon grease
1 chicken bouillon cube
1 medium onion, chopped
2 teaspoons minced garlic
2 teaspoons hot sauce (optional)

Thaw collards and pat dry. Melt butter in skillet over medium heat. Break up bouillon, add to skillet, and stir until blended. Add onion, garlic, hot sauce and collards; cook until soft.

Boiled Collard Greens

2½ pounds collard greens
6 to 8 thick slices bacon, diced
¼ cup chopped onion
2 teaspoons salt
Crushed red pepper
Dash seasoned salt
½ teaspoon Cajun seasoning (optional)

Wash greens in about 3 changes of water, until no sediment can be felt. Cut-out thick stalks and thick veins. Roll leaves and chop coarsely. Cook bacon and onion in a skillet. Combine greens, bacon and onion in a large pot with water to cover. Boil until greens are tender. Season with remaining ingredients before serving.

Yellow Squash and Cheese

4 pounds yellow squash, sliced
4 tablespoons butter, divided
1 large sweet onion, finely chopped
2 cloves garlic, minced
2½ cups soft breadcrumbs, divided
1¼ cups shredded Parmesan cheese, divided
1 cup shredded Cheddar cheese
½ cup freshly chopped chives and parsley
1 (8-ounce) container sour cream
1 teaspoon salt
1 teaspoon pepper
2 large eggs, beaten
¼ teaspoon garlic salt

Cook squash in boiling water until tender; drain well. Melt 2 tablespoons butter in a large skillet; add onion and garlic. Cook until onions are tender. Stir in half of breadcrumbs, half of Parmesan cheese, all of Cheddar cheese, parsley, sour cream, salt, pepper and eggs. Spoon into a baking dish. Melt remaining butter with remaining breadcrumbs, remaining Parmesan cheese and garlic salt. Sprinkle over top of casserole. Bake, uncovered, at 350° for 35 minutes.

©Taste of the Mountain Food Fair

Taste of the Mountain Food Fair
Monteagle • Second Monday in March

Held at the National Guard Armory, "everything from possum to pâté" is featured fare as restaurants, caterers, and bakeries from the Mountain provide samples of their specialties.

www.monteaglechamber.com

Pineapple Beets

2 tablespoons brown sugar
1 tablespoon cornstarch
¼ teaspoon salt
1 can diced pineapple with syrup
1 tablespoon butter
1 tablespoon lemon juice
1 can sliced beets, drained

In a saucepan over medium heat, combine brown sugar, cornstarch, and salt. Stir in pineapple with syrup. Cook, stirring constantly, until mixture is thickened and bubbly. Add butter, lemon juice, and drained sliced beets. Heat thoroughly, 4 to 6 minutes.

Buttered Yellow Squash & Zucchini

3 medium yellow summer squash
2 medium zucchini
1 cup sliced carrots
½ cup sliced mushrooms
2 tablespoons olive oil
1 tablespoon butter
½ cup Parmesan cheese

In a skillet over medium-high heat, combine vegetables and oil; cook, stirring constantly, until tender but still a little crisp. Add butter and top with cheese.

Three-Bean Baked Beans

1 large onion, chopped
¼ cup extra virgin olive oil
1 tablespoon minced garlic
1 can baked beans
1 can kidney beans
1 can pinto beans
½ cup finely diced tomatoes
1 bell pepper, minced
¼ cup brown sugar

Add all ingredients to a glass baking dish. Stir well and bake at 275° at least 2 hours or more.

Meaty Baked Beans

½ pound ground sausage
3 cans pork & beans
1 can tomato paste
½ cup barbecue sauce
¼ cup brown sugar
1/3 cup minced apples (optional)
½ cup chopped onion
¼ cup hot sauce (optional)
8 bacon strips

Brown and drain sausage. In a baking dish or pan, combine sausage with remaining ingredients except bacon. Top with bacon strips. Bake 2 to 3 hours at 300°.

White Beans & Cornbread

1 (2-pound) bag white beans
1 left-over ham bone
1 onion, chopped

1 teaspoon minced garlic
½ teaspoon black pepper
Salt and pepper

Sort beans and remove any rocks or bad beans. Soak remaining beans overnight. Rinse beans with water and place in large stockpot. Add ham bone, onion, garlic, pepper, and water to cover. Cook over high heat until boiling. Cover and reduce heat to medium low. Do not over-stir. Salt and pepper to taste when tender. Serve hot with onions and cornbread.

Farmer's Market
Nashville

©Kenneth Keith Stilger • Image from BigStockPhoto.com

Corn Pudding

3 eggs, beaten
3 tablespoons sugar
1 tablespoon brown sugar
1 large dash salt
1 large dash black pepper
½ cup butter
2 cans creamed corn
¼ cup finely crushed Ritz crackers

Mix all ingredients, except crushed Ritz crackers, in glass baking dish; bake at 300° 30 to 40 minutes or until set. Top pudding with crackers last 5 minutes of cooking. Serve hot.

Country-Fried Cream Corn

4 tablespoons butter
2 cans whole-kernel corn, drained
1 can cream-style corn
1 can green chilies, drained
½ cup half and half
1 teaspoon chili powder
1 teaspoon allspice
1 large dash salt
1 large dash pepper
1 large dash crushed red pepper
⅓ cup chopped onion

In a large skillet, melt butter; add corn. Cook to brown edges of corn. Add remaining ingredients; mix well. Simmer until most of the moisture is cooked off. Delicious served with freshly sliced tomatoes.

Crockpot, Casserole & One-Skillet Dishes

Crockpot Beef and Beans

2 pounds ground beef
1 large onion, chopped
1 can red beans
1 can black beans
1 can pinto beans
1 large can tomatoes with chilies
1 large can diced tomatoes
1 package taco seasoning mix
1 package ranch dressing mix
¼ cup brown sugar

Brown meat and onion; drain. Combine all ingredients in a crockpot and cook on high 4 to 5 hours.

Crockpot Beefy Mac and Cheese

2 pounds ground beef
1 cup diced onion
3 cups shredded pepper jack cheese
1 can diced tomatoes and green chilies
1 jar cheese dip
12 ounces dried elbow macaroni
1½ cups water
1 packet taco seasoning

In a large skillet, brown ground beef and onion; drain. Combine all ingredients in crockpot. Cover, cook on high until noodles are soft. Add more milk to thin, if necessary. Add additional cheese if desired.

Crockpot Hot Lunch

1 onion, chopped
2 pounds ground beef, browned and drained
6 medium potatoes, cubed
1 can red beans
1 can tomato soup
Salt, pepper, and garlic powder to taste

Combine all ingredients in a large crockpot. Cover and cook on low 7 to 9 hours stirring only as needed.

Crockpot Stroganoff

2 pounds round steak, 1-inch pieces
¼ cup flour
½ teaspoon black pepper
½ teaspoon salt
1 teaspoon minced garlic
Olive or vegetable oil
3 tablespoons butter
1 small onion, chopped
1 tablespoon soy sauce
2 beef bouillon cubes
1 can cream of mushroom soup
⅔ cup water
2 cups elbow macaroni or favorite noodle

Mix steak chunks with flour, pepper, salt and garlic; brown in a skillet with oil. Combine browned steak with remaining ingredients in a crockpot and cook on low 5 hours. Add milk or water as needed.

Crockpot Pulled Pork

1 pork roast
Juice of 1 lemon
1 small onion, chopped
1 tablespoon sugar
1 tablespoon brown sugar
1 bottle barbecue sauce

Place pork roast in crockpot; add remaining ingredients. If necessary, add water to cover. Cook on high 6 to 8 hours or low 10 to 12 hours or until roast easily falls apart. Drain, discarding liquid, and pull meat into shredded pieces. Add a bit more of your favorite barbecue sauce, if desired.

Bloomin' Barbeque & Bluegrass
Sevierville • May

The Bloomin' Barbeque & Bluegrass festival features the Tennessee State Championship Barbecue Competition where an estimated 2,832 pounds of meat are cooked by teams from across the United States. More than 20,000 attendees enjoy world-class bluegrass music, arts and crafts, kids games and the one and only Mountain Soul Vocal Competition.

http://www.bloominbbq.com/

Bloomie the Pig welcomes you to
Bloomin' Barbeque & Bluegrass
Sevierville

Tennessee

Crockpot Chicken and Dumplings

3 chicken breasts, bone-in with skin
3 cups water
1 chicken bouillon cube
3 to 4 stalks celery, diced
3 to 4 carrots, diced

1 small onion, minced
½ tablespoon salt
½ tablespoon pepper
2 cans small biscuits

Add chicken, water, bouillon cube, celery, carrots, and onions to crockpot; salt and pepper to taste. Cook 2 hours on high. When veggies are tender, de-bone chicken and remove skin. Add water as needed and additional seasonings as desired. About 30 minutes before serving, open canned biscuits and cut each biscuit into 4 to 6 small pieces. Add pieces to crockpot one at a time pushing each piece below broth. Cook covered on high until dumplings puff and swell up. Try not to over-stir. Use inexpensive canned biscuits, not the huge, flaky ones.

Crockpot Barbecue

2 to 3 pound boneless pork roast
¾ cup dried minced onion
1 bottle barbecue sauce
¼ cup honey
⅓ cup water
2 tablespoons yellow mustard
½ teaspoon apple vinegar

Cube roast into fist-size pieces; place in a greased crockpot. Add onion, barbecue sauce, honey, water, mustard and vinegar. Cover and cook on low 6 to 8 hours. After about 3 hours, begin to break meat up with a fork. Serve hot over buns with slaw and baked beans.

Crockpot Sweet and Sour Pork

1½ pounds boneless pork chops, cubed
1 can pineapple chunks
½ cup sweet and sour sauce
1 tablespoon soy sauce
¼ teaspoon ground ginger
Salt and pepper
½ teaspoon soy sauce

Combine all in a crockpot and cook on low 5 hours. Serve with rice, noodles or Oriental noodles.

Chattanooga National Cemetery
Chattanooga

©Donald Kinsey • Image from BigStockPhoto.com

Tennessee

Crockpot Pineapple Chicken & Rice

4 bonless skinless chicken breasts
1 (8-ounce) can crushed pineapple
1 can water chestnuts
1½ cups water
1 cup rice

Combine all ingredients in a crockpot and cook on high 3 to 4 hours or on low 6 to 8 hours.

Crockpot Red Beans & Sausage

2 to 3 cans red kidney beans
2 cups smoked sausage, thinly sliced
1 large bell pepper, chopped
1 large onion, chopped
2 stalks celery, chopped
1 carrot, diced
1 tablespoon hot sauce
1 tablespoon minced garlic
¼ teaspoon thyme
¼ teaspoon sage
½ cup red wine
2 tablespoons Chow Chow

Put everything in crockpot on low heat; add water to cover. Cook covered 6 to 10 hours. Add more water, if needed. Serve over rice. (Chow Chow can usually be found in the grocery store near the relish. If you do not have any on-hand, a hot relish or salsa can be substituted.)

Almond Turkey or Chicken Casserole

4 cups cubed cooked turkey or chicken
1 cup diced celery
1 cup broccoli pieces
1 yellow bell pepper, diced
⅔ cup sliced almonds
1½ cups mayonnaise
1 teaspoon salt
½ teaspoon dried thyme
¼ teaspoon pepper
1 cup crushed potato chips or crushed crackers
1 cup shredded Cheddar cheese

Combine meat, vegetables, almonds, mayonnaise and seasoning in a bowl; pour into a greased 2-quart baking dish. Top with potato chips. Bake, uncovered, at 450° for 15 minutes or until heated through. Top with cheese; serve hot.

Giles County Gobbler Gala and Tennessee Governor's One Shot Turkey Hunt
Pulaski • 2nd weekend in April

Giles County is host to the Governor's One Shot Turkey Hunt — an annual event attracting turkey hunters from throughout the country. In addition to the Turkey Hunt, there are craft and food vendors, live entertainment, a turkey roll competition, lots of fun stuff for the kids, and a "Run Turkey Run" 5k run/walk. This outstanding event commences with a Gobbler Gala/One-Shot Banquet featuring more live entertainment.

www.gilescountytourism.com

© Don King

Nacho Chicken Bake Casserole

1½ cups cubed cooked chicken
1 cup crushed **Doritos**
1 can cream of chicken soup
½ cup freshly sliced mushrooms
⅓ cup drained black olive slices or pieces
¼ cup sour cream
2 tablespoons milk
1 tablespoon chopped green chilies
½ teaspoon finely chopped jalapeño pepper
¼ cup shredded part-skim mozzarella cheese
¼ cup shredded Cheddar cheese

In a bowl, combine all ingredients except cheeses. Combine cheeses; mix half into chicken mixture. Spoon chicken mix into a large baking dish coated with nonstick cooking spray. Bake at 350° for 30 minutes or until bubbly. Sprinkle with remaining cheese and cook until melted. Serve hot.

Baked Cashew Chicken & Rice

1 pound boneless chicken
  breasts, chopped
1 medium onion, sliced
1 celery stalk, chopped
2 cups chopped frozen broccoli
1¾ cups boiling water
1 cup uncooked long-grain rice
½ cup chopped mushrooms
1 chicken bouillon cube
½ tablespoon ground ginger
½ teaspoon pepper
1 cup salted cashews, divided

In a large bowl, combine all ingredients except half the cashews. Transfer to a greased baking dish. Cover and bake at 375° 45 minutes or until rice is tender and chicken is cooked. Sprinkle with remaining cashews, before serving.

Chicken & Sausage Casserole

½ pound smoked sausage, chopped
3 chicken breasts, cubed
1 beef bouillon cube
½ cup water
¼ cup chili powder
2 teaspoons ground cumin
1 teaspoon jalapeño, minced
½ teaspoon salt

¼ cup butter, melted
1 onion, diced
½ tablespoon minced garlic
2 red bell peppers, diced
1 can green chilies
1 can diced tomatoes
1 can tomato paste
2 cans chili beans, drained

Brown sausage and chicken pieces in a skillet with some oil. Dissolve bouillon cube in water. Drain meat and combine with bouillon, and remaining ingredients; pour into a large greased casserole dish. Bake at 350° for 30 minutes.

Taco Casserole

1 pound ground beef
1 cup medium salsa
½ cup mayonnaise
2 teaspoons chili powder
2 teaspoons cumin powder
1 teaspoon hot sauce

2 to 3 cups crushed tortilla chips
1 cup shredded colby cheese
1 cup shredded Monterey Jack
1 can diced tomatoes, drained
2 cups shredded lettuce

In a saucepan, brown ground beef; drain. Stir in salsa, mayonnaise, chili powder, cumin and hot sauce. In an ungreased 2-quart baking dish, layer half of the meat mixture, top with ½ chips and ½ cheeses. Repeat layers. Bake, uncovered, at 350° for 20 to 25 minutes or until heated through. Top with tomato and lettuce just before serving.

Swiss Steak Bake

2 pounds round steak, sliced
¾ cup all-purpose flour, divided
2 teaspoons salt
¾ teaspoon pepper
½ teaspoon garlic salt
3 tablespoons vegetable oil
1 garlic clove, minced
2 cups chopped green bell pepper
1 cup chopped celery
1 cup chopped onion
2 cans diced tomatoes, undrained
1 cup beef broth
1 tablespoon soy sauce
¼ cup cold water

Pound meat to tenderize, if needed. In a large zip-close bag, combine ½ cup flour, salt, pepper and garlic salt. Add beef and toss to coat. In a large skillet, brown meat in heated oil. In a large casserole dish, combine beef mix with garlic, bell pepper, celery, onion, tomatoes (with juice), broth, soy sauce and salt and pepper to taste. Cover and bake at 325° for 2 hours. Remove from oven. Drain excess juice into a small saucepan. Stir water and remaining ¼ cup flour into juices. Bring to a boil over medium heat until thickened. Pour over steak.

Shepherd's Pie Casserole

1 pound lean ground beef
½ cup chopped onion
½ cup chopped celery
1 can condensed vegetable soup
½ teaspoon dried thyme
1½ teaspoons pepper
1 teaspoon salt
3 cups cooked mashed potatoes
1 cup shredded cheese

Brown ground beef with onion and celery; drain. Mix with vegetable soup, thyme, pepper and salt. Place into a casserole dish and spread mashed potatoes evenly on top. Bake 30 minutes at 350°. Sprinkle shredded cheese on top and continue to cook until cheese has melted.

Baked Spaghetti

1 (16-ounce) box spaghetti
1 pound ground beef
1 medium onion, chopped
2 cans tomato sauce
1 spaghetti seasoning packet
½ teaspoon seasoned salt

2 eggs, beaten
⅓ cup grated Parmesan cheese
5 tablespoons butter, melted
2 cups small-curd cottage cheese
4 cups shredded mozzarella cheese

Cook spaghetti according to box directions; drain. In a large skillet, brown ground beef and onion; drain. Stir in tomato sauce, spaghetti seasoning, and seasoned salt. In a large bowl, combine eggs, Parmesan cheese, butter and drained noodles; mix well. Spoon half the noodle mixture in a greased 9x13-inch baking dish. Top with half of the cottage cheese, half the meat sauce and half the mozzarella cheese. Repeat layers ending with cheese. Cover and bake at 350° for 30 minutes. Uncover and cook an additional 30 minutes. Allow to cool about 5 minutes before serving.

Hodge Podge Casserole

1 (8-ounce) package elbow macaroni
1 pound ground beef
⅓ cup minced onion
¾ teaspoon salt
1 zucchini, chopped
1 can whole-kernel corn, undrained
1 cup tomato sauce
½ cup grated cheese

Cook noodles and drain. Brown beef and onion; drain then add salt. Place meat in large casserole dish and top with zucchini and corn (with liquid). Add noodles, tomato sauce and cheese. Bake at 325° uncovered for 45 minutes. Serve hot.

Veggie Beef Cheese Bake

1 pound ground beef
3 medium potatoes, sliced with peel
3 medium carrots, sliced
3 celery stalks, chopped
1 onion, chopped
1 can green beans, drained
1 teaspoon dried thyme, divided
1 teaspoon salt, divided
1 teaspoon pepper, divided
1 can tomatoes and green chilies
1 cup shredded Cheddar cheese

Brown ground beef in your favorite seasonings. In a large casserole dish sprayed with nonstick spray, layer half of the potatoes, carrots, celery, onions and green beans. Crumble half the beef over vegetables. Sprinkle with ½ teaspoon each of thyme, salt and pepper. Repeat layers. Top with tomatoes and chilies. Cover and bake at 400° 20 minutes. Reduce heat to 350° and bake about 1 hour longer or until vegetables are tender. Top with cheese and serve hot.

Jim Bales Place
Great Smoky Mountains National Park

© Jerry Whaley

Easy Tater Tot Casserole

1½ pounds lean ground beef
1 onion, finely chopped
1 red bell pepper, finely chopped
1 teaspoon garlic salt
1 teaspoon pepper
1 (32-ounce) package tater tots
1 can cream of mushroom soup
1 can cream of celery soup
1 small can French-fried onion rings

In a large skillet, cook ground beef with onion, bell pepper, garlic salt, and pepper; drain and spread into the bottom of a greased 9x13-inch baking dish. Layer tater tots over meat. Combine soups and pour over tots. Lightly cover with foil and bake 1 hour at 350°. During the last 10 minutes of cooking, remove foil and top with onion rings.

Chili Biscuit Casserole

½ pound ground beef
½ pound ground pork
1 onion, chopped
1 green bell pepper, chopped
1 can chili beans
1 (8-ounce) can tomato sauce
1 can tomato paste
2 tablespoons chili powder
1 tablespoon hot pepper sauce
1 can biscuits
2 cups crushed corn chips
1 cup shredded Cheddar cheese

In a skillet, brown beef, pork, onions, and bell peppers; drain. Add in beans, tomato sauce, tomato paste, chili powder and hot pepper sauce. Cook on medium high for about 30 minutes, then reduce heat to low. Simmer, uncovered, until mixture thickens. Separate biscuits and arrange them in the bottom of a pie plate, pressing into bottom and up the sides. Spoon ground beef mixture into crust. Bake pie, uncovered, at 375° about 30 minutes. Top with chips and cheese; cook about 10 minutes to melt cheese.

Cosby Ramp Festival
Cosby • May

The ramp (allium tricoccum), or wild leek, belongs to the same family as chives and garlic and is native to eastern North America. Long used by Native Americans for medicinal purposes and early settlers in cooking, the ramp still is an integral rite of spring in regional cooking. The flavor is similar to that of garlic and onion, but more pronounced and musty. The ramp has been called "the sweetest tasting and vilest smelling vegetable in Nature's bounty." The Cosby Ramp Festival has been held every May since 1954 and includes a recipe contest featuring fare such as Green Eggs & Ramps and BBQ Chicken served with Ramps. Other events include a Maid of Ramps contest, Appalachian crafts, country, gospel, bluegrass and rock & roll music.

www.cosbyrampfestival.org

Ramp & Sausage Casserole

1 pound pork sausage, browned
4 eggs, beaten
2 cups milk
1 tablespoon minced garlic
1 teaspoon salt
1 teaspoon pepper
8 small potatoes, sliced
15 ramps, chopped
2 cups shredded Cheddar cheese

In skillet, brown sausage and drain grease. In a bowl, combine eggs, milk, garlic, salt and pepper. In a large greased baking dish, layer ½ potatoes, ½ sausage and ½ chopped ramps. Repeat layers then gently pour egg and milk mixture over layers. Bake at 350° until potatoes are tender, 30 to 40 minutes. Before removing from oven, top with cheese. Cook until cheese is melted.

© Newport Plain Talk

Pork Chop Dutch Oven Bake

8 pork chops, medium sliced
⅓ cup all-purpose flour
¼ cup butter or margarine
1 teaspoon salt
1 teaspoon pepper
2 cups apple juice, divided
2 pounds small red potatoes
1 onion, thick sliced
2 carrots, sliced
6 cups shredded cabbage

Coat pork chops in flour; reserve excess flour. In a large Dutch oven, melt butter over medium-high heat. Brown chops on both sides; season with salt and pepper. Remove and set aside. Stir reserved flour into pan; cook and stir until a paste forms. Gradually whisk in 1½ cups apple juice and blend until smooth. Return chops to Dutch oven; cover and bake at 350° 30 minutes. Add potatoes, onions, carrots and remaining apple juice. Cover and bake 30 minutes longer. Top with cabbage; cover and bake 1 to 1½ hours or until pork chops are tender, basting occasionally with juices.

Pork

Cajun Battered Beer Chops

Family pack thin-sliced boneless pork chops
1 box fish batter mix
1 beer
Soy sauce
2 tablespoons Cajun Seasoning
Salt and pepper

Prepare batter as directed on box but replace liquid with beer. Rub chops with remaining ingredients to coat. Dip each chop in batter and cook in hot oil until golden brown.

Glazed Pork Chops

4 boneless pork chops
¼ teaspoon freshly ground pepper
Olive oil
⅓ cup apple juice
½ cup cranberry sauce
2 tablespoons honey
⅓ cup orange juice
¼ teaspoon ground ginger
⅛ teaspoon ground nutmeg

Evenly coat each chop lightly with pepper and brown in hot skillet with olive oil. When chops begin to brown, add apple juice. Cover tightly and cook on low heat until chops are just done. Apple juice should be almost cooked dry. In a small bowl, while chops are cooking, combine cranberry sauce, honey, orange juice, ginger and nutmeg. Brush over chops while they cook. Evenly coat and allow to glaze. Serve hot.

Balsamic Pork Chops with Cherry Tomatoes & Rice

10 thin-sliced boneless pork chops
1½ cups balsamic vinaigrette dressing
1 box seasoned rice
Olive oil
½ cup chopped shallots or onions
1 cup sliced cherry tomatoes
Parsley

Place chops in large bowl with dressing. Cover and refrigerate at least 2 hours. Cook rice as directed on box. Remove chops from marinade and brown in a hot non-stick skillet with oil. In another skillet, brown shallots in oil. Add marinade from chops and simmer. Before removing from heat stir in tomatoes. Serve pork chops over seasoned rice topped with tomato mix and parsley.

Honey Pork Chops

4 (1-inch thick) pork chops
¼ cup soy sauce
¼ cup lemon juice
2 tablespoons honey
½ teaspoon garlic powder
¼ teaspoon pepper

Place chops in a shallow glass dish. Combine remaining ingredients and mix well. Pour over chops. Cover tightly and refrigerate several hours, overnight if possible. Bake chops in marinade in glass dish at 350° or cook over medium heat on the stove top until done.

Honey-Pecan Pork with Sweet Onion Sauce

4 pork chops
Oil
4 tablespoons flour
½ teaspoon salt
¼ teaspoon ground black pepper
Butter
¼ cup honey
¼ cup chopped pecans

Sweet Onion Sauce:
⅔ cup light corn syrup
1½ tablespoons minced white onion
1 tablespoon red wine vinegar
2 teaspoons white distilled vinegar
1 teaspoon balsamic vinegar
1 teaspoon brown sugar
1 teaspoon garlic powder
½ teaspoon lemon juice
1 pinch salt
1 pinch black pepper

Brush chops with oil. Combine flour, salt and pepper; dredge chops in flour mixture. In a skillet, cook chops in melted butter over medium-high heat; brown both sides. Stir in honey and pecans. In a small saucepan combine Sweet Onion Sauce ingredients and heat to a quick simmer. Stir and remove from heat. If you like a lot of sauce, double the Sweet Onion Sauce. Serve Honey-Pecan Pork Chops with Sweet Onion Sauce on side.

Blue Cheese Pork Chops with Mixed Green Salad

4 boneless pork chops
4 teaspoons olive oil plus more for coating chops
¾ cup soft breadcrumbs
½ cup crumbled blue cheese
3 tablespoons Wheat Chex cereal, crushed
2 tablespoons finely chopped green onion
¼ teaspoon salt
¼ teaspoon pepper

Place pork on a broiler pan and brush with a light amount of olive oil. Broil about 4 inches from heat 5 to 8 minutes. While chops are cooking, combine breadcrumbs, blue cheese, cereal, onion, salt, pepper and 4 tablespoons olive oil in a bowl. Remove and turn chops. Spread crumb mixture evenly on top and some on sides of chops. Return to broiler 1 to 2 minutes until crumbs brown and cheese melts. Serve over mixed green salad with blue cheese dressing. If you do not like blue cheese, try your favorite cheese and dressing.

George Dickel Tennessee Whisky Pork Chops

4 to 6 boneless pork chops
4 tablespoons Dijon mustard
4 tablespoons George Dickel Whisky
4 tablespoons brown sugar
1 teaspoon black pepper
2 tablespoons soy sauce
1 tablespoon minced green onion
Oil

In a bowl, combine mustard, whisky, brown sugar, pepper, soy sauce and green onion. Place chops and sauce in a zip-close bag. Coat evenly by rolling in hands; chill overnight. Remove chops from marinade. Cook in a skillet with hot oil over medium heat. Add about 3 tablespoons of the remaining marinade and cook chops 4 to 5 minutes on each side. Serve hot.

Pork Gyros with Cucumber Sauce

1½ pounds boneless pork
5 tablespoons olive oil
2 tablespoons Dijon mustard
½ cup lemon juice
1 tablespoon minced garlic
1½ teaspoons oregano
1½ teaspoons onion powder
2 pita loaves
Onion slices

Cucumber Sauce:

1 cup plain low fat yogurt
1 cucumber, peeled, seeded and diced
½ teaspoon garlic powder
½ teaspoon pepper
½ teaspoon dill

Cut pork crosswise into thin pieces and combine in a zip-close bag with olive oil, mustard, lemon juice, garlic, oregano and onion powder. Evenly coat all pieces, seal and chill overnight, if possible. In a small bowl stir together Cucumber Sauce ingredients; cover and chill. In a pan, cook pork on high 10 to 15 minutes. Cut each pita loaf in half and gently open to form pocket. Put equal amounts pork in each half and top with Cucumber Sauce and onions.

Greek Festival

Memphis • May

Annunciation Greek Orthodox Church's Greek Festival is the place for anyone who loves Greek food or who wants to give it a try. The dinner provides a range of tastes. If you don't want to stand in line, you can order individual items at the food stands. The food includes gyros (a sandwich with lamb), spanakopita (a pastry with spinach), and souvlaki (a chicken kebab). Indulge your sweet tooth with a variety of dessert pastries including baklava (a pastry with honey and nuts). After eating, burn off the calories dancing to live Greek music.

www.memphisgreekfestival.com

©Greek Festival

Tennessee

Stuffed Pork Chops

6 pork chops, 2 inches thick
3 tablespoons hot water
1 tablespoon butter, melted
1 cup cornbread stuffing mix
1 can whole-kernel corn, drained

2 tablespoons minced red bell pepper
2 tablespoons minced green onion
2 tablespoons freshly chopped basil
1/8 teaspoon black pepper
1 tablespoon water

Butterfly each chop to form a pocket for stuffing. Combine hot water, melted butter and seasoning packet from stuffing in small mixing bowl and stir. Add stuffing mix, corn, bell pepper, onion, basil, pepper, and water. Stir until all liquid is absorbed. Spoon mixture into pockets in chops. Close with wooden picks or small skewers. Cook lightly covered with foil in a 375° oven 30 to 40 minutes or until juice runs clear. Baste with drippings as needed.

Fried Seasoned Breaded Pork Chops

4 bone-in pork chops
1/8 teaspoon black pepper plus
    more for chops
1/2 cup flour
1/2 teaspoon Cajun seasoning
1/2 teaspoon salt

1/2 teaspoon paprika
1 egg, slightly beaten
1/3 cup milk
1 teaspoon Worcestershire sauce
1/2 cup crumbled Ritz crackers
Oil

Sprinkle both sides of each chop with black pepper; set aside. Combine flour, Cajun seasoning, salt, paprika, and 1/8 teaspoon pepper; mix. In another small bowl, combine egg, milk and Worcestershire sauce. Coat chops with seasoned flour; dip in egg mixture, and coat with cracker crumbs. Repeat process, if needed. In a skillet, heat oil and cook chops on both sides until golden brown. Drain on a paper towel, then serve hot.

Grilled Pineapple Pork Chops

4 thick bone-in pork chops
2 tablespoons olive oil plus more
   for coating chops
½ fresh pineapple, peeled, cored
   and sliced
1 can green chilies

4 small green onions, thinly sliced
3 tablespoons fresh lime juice
2 tablespoons finely chopped fresh
   cilantro leaves
2 tablespoons maple syrup
½ teaspoon salt

Pineapple Marinade:

2 tablespoons packed brown sugar
2 tablespoons salt
1 cup water
¾ cup pineapple juice

For marinade, stir together brown sugar, salt and 1 cup water in a small saucepan. Bring to boil, stirring occasionally, until salt and sugar are dissolved. Remove from heat. Stir in pineapple juice and cool. Combine chops and marinade in a covered bowl and chill at least 2 hours or more. Remove, pat dry and brush with olive oil. Grill chops over direct heat 12 to 16 minutes. In a skillet, combine pineapple and remaining ingredients. Cook until juice reduces down. Place pineapple slices on grill to add grill marks. Serve with chops while hot.

Dijon Cinnamon Apple Pork Chops

4 to 6 boneless pork chops, ½-inch thick
Olive oil
¼ teaspoon black pepper plus
    more for chops
3 tablespoons Dijon mustard
½ tablespoon cinnamon
2 tablespoons Italian dressing
¼ teaspoon thyme
Dash cumin powder
1 onion, thinly sliced
½ cup apple juice
1 cup chopped apples

Brown chops on both sides in a skillet with a bit of olive oil and black pepper. In a bowl, combine mustard, cinnamon, Italian dressing, pepper, thyme and cumin. Spread over each chop; continue to brown and cook. Stir in onion. Add apple juice and chopped apples. Cook and stir over medium heat until juices run clear. Serve hot.

Broiled Pork Chop Mole

4 pork chops, ¾-inch thick
2 tablespoons ketchup
1 teaspoon unsweetened cocoa
½ teaspoon garlic salt
¼ teaspoon cinnamon
¼ teaspoon chili powder
Pinch cayenne pepper
1 to 2 tablespoons water

Stir together ketchup, cocoa, garlic salt, cinnamon, chili powder and cayenne pepper. Stir in water until smooth. Place chops on broiler rack, brush lightly with mole sauce. Broil close to heat for 4 minutes. Turn, brush with sauce, and broil other side about 4 minutes more. Additional mole sauce can be made to serve on the side. Serve hot.

Beale Street Barbecue Ribs

3 to 4 pounds pork spareribs
½ cup soy sauce
½ cup yellow mustard
¼ cup apple cider vinegar
¼ cup water
1 teaspoon salt
1 teaspoon black pepper
3 to 4 garlic cloves, crushed
¼ cup honey
Hot sauce to taste

Combine soy sauce, mustard, vinegar, water, salt, pepper, and garlic. Marinate ribs 1 to 2 hours. Combine honey and hot sauce. If using the oven, place marinade in bottom of pan, baste meat with honey mixture and bake at 400°. If using grill, boil marinade (on stove or in microwave) then use it to baste ribs while grilling. Baste with honey mixture the last 20 minutes of cooking. Ribs are done when bone pulls away from meat with ease.

Memphis in May World Championship Barbecue Cooking Contest
Memphis • May

Called the "Super Bowl of Swine" and the "Largest Pork Barbecue Cooking Contest on the Planet," this world-class event is held each May at Tom Lee Park on the banks of the Mississippi River. The focus is three days of intense competition where teams eat, sleep, and live barbecue— vying for prizes and bragging rights. More than 90,000 barbecue lovers from around the world gather to sample and compete with sauces, rubs, and all things pork and barbecue. There is even a Ms. Piggie competition where grown men don snouts and tutus.

www.memphisinmay.org

Serving up Barbecue at
Memphis in May

©Memphis in May

©Memphis in May

Fried Pork Quesadillas

1 pound pork chops, small cubes
¾ cup flour
1 tablespoon ground cumin
1 tablespoon chili powder
1 teaspoon cayenne pepper
2 eggs, lightly beaten
⅓ cup milk
¼ cup olive oil
2 cups shredded Monterey Jack cheese
⅔ cup chopped tomatoes
2 tablespoons lime juice
Salsa
8 flour tortillas
Sour cream

In a shallow plate, combine flour, cumin, chili powder, and cayenne pepper. In a bowl, combine eggs and milk; mix well. Dip pork in egg mix then dredge in flour mixture. In large skillet, cook breaded pork in hot oil over medium-high heat until golden and pork is cooked through. Drain on paper towels. Put equal amounts of pork, shredded cheese, tomatoes, lime juice and a bit of salsa in center of each tortilla and fold over. In a large skillet with nonstick cooking spray, brown each shell on both sides allowing cheese to melt inside. Top with salsa and sour cream. (Also delicious with left-over barbecue or unbreaded pork chops.)

Pork Parmesan

4 boneless pork steaks or chops
1 egg, beaten
½ cup milk
1 cup Italian-seasoned
   breadcrumbs
⅓ cup olive oil
10 slices mozzarella cheese
1 cup spaghetti sauce
1 teaspoon garlic powder
½ cup Parmesan cheese

Combine egg and milk. Dip pork in milk mixture then dredge in breadcrumbs. Brown both sides in skillet with olive oil until golden. Sprinkle more breadcrumbs, if needed, as chops are cooking. Arrange chops in a baking dish and top with mozzarella cheese. Pour sauce over cheese, sprinkle with garlic powder and Parmesan cheese. Bake at 350° for about 15 minutes or until warmed through. Top with additional mozzarella cheese before serving, if desired. Serve hot.

Grilled Seasoned Pork Ribs

2 slabs pork ribs
Worcestershire sauce
1 cup ketchup
½ cup yellow mustard
¼ cup Worcestershire sauce
¼ cup vinegar
2 teaspoons paprika
2 teaspoons chili powder
1 medium onion, chopped
1 teaspoon black pepper

Marinate ribs in Worcestershire sauce. Cut each slab of ribs into about four sections. Place ribs membrane (removed) side-down over direct high heat for about 15 minutes. Flip and grill other side for about 15 minutes to brown each side. Combine remaining ingredients and baste. Wrap in many layers of foil and grill for about 2 hours turning often over medium low heat.

Carolina Pork Barbecue

1 pork butt (shoulder)
¼ cup hot sauce
1 gallon apple cider vinegar
1 tablespoon crushed red pepper
1¼ cups (10 ounces) Worcestershire sauce

The key, according to my pit-master friends, to good Carolina Pork Barbecue is apple cider vinegar, lots of smoke, plenty of time and a nice thin barbecue sauce to pour over it before you eat! This is a simple recipe.

Place pork butt in a deep bowl. Mix all remaining ingredients together and marinate pork in refrigerator several hours. Remove pork and boil marinade to use as a basting sauce for the meat. Cook the pork long and slow. Use indirect heat over a real wood fire, preferably hickory. Temperature should be around 220°, and it takes at least 1½ hours per pound, or until internal temperature reaches 180 to 190°. Pull with a fork and serve as quickly as possible.

Jack Black Barbecued Ribs

2 slabs pork ribs, membrane removed
Worcestershire sauce

Rub:

2 tablespoons paprika
1 tablespoon garlic powder
1 tablespoon salt
1 tablespoon Italian seasoning
1 tablespoon chili powder
½ tablespoon brown sugar

Sauce:

1 cup apple cider vinegar
⅓ to ½ cup Jack Daniels Black Label
4 tablespoons yellow mustard
1 cup cold water
2 tablespoons vegetable oil
2 tablespoons brown sugar
1½ teaspoons red pepper flakes
½ teaspoon cayenne pepper

Brush each slab evenly with a light coat of Worcestershire sauce. Combine Rub ingredients in a bowl. Rub into each slab of ribs on both sides. Wrap ribs with foil or cling wrap. Refrigerate overnight, if possible. In a bowl, combine Sauce ingredients. Remove ribs from foil; grill, covered, using high heat and wood chips. Brown each side, then baste with half of the barbecue sauce. Wrap each slab in foil. Grill using indirect heat, if possible, or low heat for 20 minutes on both sides. This seals in juices. Remove from foil and baste again. Grill an additional 10 to 15 minutes. Rib meat should pull away from bone with ease. Serve hot.

Sorghum & Pepper Pork Roast

3 to 4 pound pork roast
2 tablespoons salt
½ cup sorghum syrup
¼ cup cranberry juice
¼ cup lemon-lime soda
1 tablespoon thyme
½ teaspoon garlic powder
Salt and pepper, to taste

Place roast in a large bowl and cover with water. Add 2 tablespoons salt and soak overnight if possible. Remove from salt-water brine and place in baking dish; discard brine. Combine remaining ingredients with ½ cup water; pour over roast. Turn to ensure all sides are coated. Lightly cover with foil and bake at 350° to an internal temp of 190°.

Baked Citrus Pork Tenderloin

2 pork tenderloins or 1 pork roast
½ cup fresh orange juice
⅓ cup fresh lime juice
¼ cup pineapple rum
5 cloves, minced
2 teaspoons oregano
2 teaspoons cumin
2 teaspoons salt
1 bay leaf
½ teaspoon ground black pepper

Put pork tenderloins in large glass bowl. A large roast can be cut into two pieces. Add remaining ingredients and baste. Cover and marinate in refrigerator overnight; turn often to coat evenly. Transfer pork and marinade to a glass baking pan. Cook at 325° until thermometer inserted in center of pork registers 150°. Baste as needed. Let pork rest 5 minutes before slicing.

Bacon-Wrapped Pork with Seasoned Sauce

1 pork tenderloin
Worcestershire sauce
Steak sauce
6 slices bacon, or more
Toothpicks
Salt and pepper

Seasoned Sauce:
3 tablespoons mayonnaise
3 tablespoons sour cream
1½ tablespoons Dijon mustard
½ tablespoon honey

Combine Seasoned Sauce ingredients in a small bowl; chill. Cut tenderloin in 6 equal pieces. Baste evenly with Worcestershire and steak sauce. Wrap bacon slice (or two, if desired) around each piece, and secure with a toothpick. Season with salt and pepper and spray lightly with cooking spray. Broil in oven turning to cook both sides or grill over medium-high to high heat. Remove wooden picks before serving with Seasoned Sauce on side or drizzled over.

Calypso Pork Tenderloin

1 pork tenderloin
1 cup chicken broth
½ cup orange juice
2 tablespoons dark rum
2 tablespoons lime juice
2 tablespoons brown sugar
1 clove garlic, minced
½ teaspoon salt
½ teaspoon ground ginger
¼ teaspoon ground nutmeg

Combine all ingredients including tenderloin in a covered glass dish or zip-close bag. Marinate as long as possible. Discard marinade and grill tenderloin over medium-high heat. If edges burn before inside is done wrap in foil to finish cooking. Slice and serve hot.

Grilled Honey Brats

6 bratwurst
1 bottle beer
½ cup honey
1 onion, sliced
1 green bell pepper, sliced
6 bun-length French rolls

In a large foil pan, combine brats, beer, honey, onion and peppers. Add water to cover brats. Place foil pan on grill and simmer until veggies are tender and brats begin to plump. Remove brats from juice and place on grill. Cook evenly until all sides are golden brown with grill marks. Place brats on buns and top with onion and pepper slices.

Grilled Italian Sausage and Pepper Jack

4 red bell peppers, sliced
4 green bell peppers, sliced
3 large onions, sliced
2 tablespoons minced garlic
2 tablespoons olive oil
Salt and pepper
4 pounds Italian sausage
Shredded pepper jack cheese

In large skillet, cook peppers, onions and garlic in oil until soft, about 5 minutes. Add salt and pepper to taste. Grill sausage on grill or in skillet until plumped. Cut into bun-length pieces and serve on a bun topped with veggies and pepper jack cheese.

Italian Pork Burgers

1½ pounds ground pork
½ tablespoon minced garlic
1 teaspoon grated Parmesan cheese
1 teaspoon ground black pepper
¼ teaspoon salt
Italian seasoning
2 tablespoons red wine
1 tablespoon olive oil
Provolone cheese slices

Combine pork, garlic, Parmesan, pepper, salt and Italian seasoning. Make 4 to 6 patties. Combine red wine and olive oil and baste each burger. Grill, covered, over medium-high heat for 5 minutes. Turn and cook an additional 5 minutes. Internal temperature should read 160°. Top with provolone cheese. Serve hot on bun with favorite toppings.

Holiday Baked Ham

1 half ham with bone
2-liter bottle cola
2-liter bottle ginger ale
½ cup brown sugar
Maple syrup
Maraschino cherries and pineapple chunks, for garnish

Place ham in a stockpot. Pour cola and ginger ale onto ham; add water to cover, if needed. Add brown sugar. Cook on low, covered, 2 hours. Turn off heat and allow to cool enough to transfer ham to a large baking pan. Save 3 to 4 cups liquid. Pour saved juice into bottom of pan and bake at 325° for 2 hours. Mix a small amount of maple syrup with juice and baste entire ham. Cook until golden brown. Garnish with cherries and pineapple chunks held on with toothpicks for last ½ hour of cooking.

World's First Coca-Cola Bottling Company

Chattanooga is the site of the world's first Coca-Cola bottling company. Before Coca-Cola first appeared in bottles, it was sold as a fountain drink for more than a decade, beginning in 1886. In the summer of 1899, Benjamin F. Thomas and Joseph B. Whitehead traveled to Atlanta from Chattanooga to meet with the owner of the Coca-Cola company. After much negotiation, the young attorneys signed a contract and paid $1.00 for exclusive bottling rights. With the help of a third partner, John T. Lupin, the entrepreneurs opened the first Coca-Cola bottling business.

www.chattanoogacocacola.com

Glazed Ham

Your choice of ham
2 cups water
½ cup honey
1 (6-ounce) can thawed orange juice concentrate

Place ham in pan and coat with remaining ingredients. Baste often as you cook in a 350° oven. Add more honey to top of ham towards end of cooking. Cook until inserted meat thermometer reads 150° or to the cooked ham reading. Cover with foil if edges burn.

Ham & Cream Cheese Crescents

2 cans refrigerated crescent rolls
Mozzarella cheese slices
1 pound thin-shaved deli ham
½ (8-ounce) package cream cheese, softened
3 tablespoons mayonnaise
1 tablespoon Dijon mustard
Salt and pepper to taste

Separate crescent rolls into triangles; place on waxed paper. Place a slice of cheese over each, then spread a thin layer of cream cheese over that. Divide ham evenly onto each triangle. Gently roll-up to form a stuffed crescent. Bake at 375° on a nonstick cookie sheet 10 to 15 minutes until golden brown. In small bowl, combine mayonnaise, mustard, salt and pepper. Serve sauce on the side.

Apple-Mustard Glazed Ham

1 cup apple jelly or apple butter
1 tablespoon Dijon mustard
1 tablespoon lemon juice
½ teaspoon ground nutmeg
½ teaspoon cinnamon
1 fully cooked ham, bone-in or out
1 apple, thinly sliced (French fry-style)
Apple juice

In a bowl, combine jelly or apple butter, mustard, lemon juice, nutmeg and cinnamon. Score the surface of the ham, making diamond shaped cuts. Lay a small slice of apple in each diamond. Hold in place with a toothpick, if needed. Place ham on a rack in a shallow roasting pan. Add equal amounts of water and apple juice to cover bottom of pan 2 to 3 inches deep. Bake at 350°, uncovered, for 20 minutes per pound or until a meat thermometer reads 140°. During the last 30 minutes of baking, brush with glaze. Cover with foil using toothpicks, if needed, to keep foil off glaze.

Double Cola Barbecue Sauce

1 can **Double Cola**
1 cup ketchup
1 small onion, minced
2 tablespoons apple cider vinegar
2 tablespoons soy sauce
2 tablespoons yellow mustard
1 teaspoon ginger
1 tablespoon horseradish (optional)

Combine ingredients in a saucepan and simmer until sauce begins to thicken. Remove from heat and use as a sauce or a baste.

Honey Butter Barbecue Sauce

1 can tomato sauce
½ cup minced onion
1 tablespoon minced garlic
2 lemon slices
½ cup melted butter
½ cup honey
Salt and pepper
1 teaspoon hot sauce

Combine everything in a saucepan and simmer 10 minutes.

Barbecue Sauce

2 cups ketchup
½ cup yellow mustard
⅓ cup water
⅓ cup lemon juice
½ cup cider vinegar
2 tablespoons brown sugar
1 tablespoon chili powder
1 tablespoon celery powder
¼ cup Worcestershire sauce
1 tablespoon minced garlic

Combine everything in a saucepan and simmer 10 minutes. Cool and chill for as long as possible before using. Chill overnight if possible.

Vinegar Barbecue Sauce

2 cups water
1 cup apple cider vinegar
3 tablespoons crushed red pepper
1 tablespoon black pepper
1 tablespoon minced garlic
Salt and pepper

Combine everything in a bowl. Pour into a glass jar and place in fridge for a week.

Beef

Tortilla Meatloaf

2 pounds ground beef
1 cup crushed plain tortilla chips
1 small onion, finely minced
1 small green bell pepper, finely minced
2 eggs, beaten

⅓ cup Worcestershire sauce
¼ cup soy sauce
1 teaspoon garlic powder
1 teaspoon cumin powder
1 teaspoon black pepper

Topping:
1 can diced tomatoes and green chilies
Paprika
Black pepper

Combine all meatloaf ingredients in a large bowl and completely mix together. Form into a loaf and bake at 350° about 45 minutes. Test for firmness in the center. Before removing from oven, top with diced tomatoes and green chilies, paprika and black pepper. Cook an additional 10 to 15 minutes.

Grandma's Onion Soup Meatloaf

1½ pounds ground beef
1 envelope instant onion soup
1 egg, beaten
1 cup crushed breadcrumbs
Salt and pepper
Ketchup
½ onion, sliced

Combine beef, soup mix, egg, breadcrumbs and salt and pepper to taste. Bake in a 350° oven about an hour. Top with ketchup and onion slices and cook an additional 5 to 10 minutes.

Memphis Barbecue Meatloaf

1½ pounds ground beef
½ pound shredded pork barbecue
2 eggs, beaten
¾ cup crushed crackers
½ cup chopped onion
¼ cup bottled barbecue sauce plus additional for topping
1 tablespoon Dijon mustard
1 tablespoon Worcestershire sauce
½ teaspoon garlic powder
½ teaspoon hot pepper sauce

In a large bowl, combine all ingredients except the additional barbecue sauce for the topping. Form into a loaf and bake at 350° 1 hour. Top with additional barbecue sauce and bake 10 minutes more. Serve hot with slaw and beans.

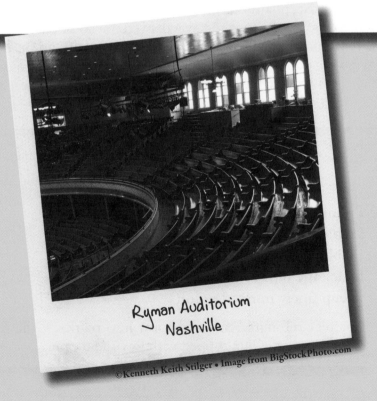

Ryman Auditorium
Nashville

©Kenneth Keith Stilger • Image from BigStockPhoto.com

Wellington Mushroom Meatloaf

1½ pounds ground beef
1 cup chopped onion, divided
1 cup chopped mushrooms, divided
1 can cream of mushroom soup, divided
1½ cups dried breadcrumbs, divided
1 tablespoon pepper
½ tablespoon minced garlic

In a large bowl, combine beef, half the onion, half the mushrooms, half the soup, half the breadcrumbs, pepper and minced garlic. Blend well and form into a loaf. Bake at 350° about 50 minutes. Remove from oven and drain excess grease, if needed. In a bowl, combine remaining onion, mushrooms and soup. Spread evenly over meatloaf and top evenly with remaining breadcrumbs. Bake to set soup mix and brown edges of breadcrumbs.

Wrapped Wellington Mushroom Meatloaf:

Follow same directions, except after baking meatloaf and before applying remaining ingredients, allow the loaf to cool to the touch. Lay a thawed phyllo or pasty dough flat on a cookie sheet. Spread the remaining ingredients, minus the breadcrumbs, on the dough; add the meatloaf and gently wrap the dough tightly around the loaf. Return to oven until dough is golden brown. You can also cut the loaf in half and make two easy-to-handle smaller loaves.

Taco Burgers

1 pound ground beef
1 tablespoon minced garlic
1 tablespoon hot sauce
1 package taco seasoning
¼ cup finely minced onion

Combine all ingredients and form into patties. Grill, fry or bake. Serve on a bun topped with favorite toppings.

Pan-Cooked Sauce Burgers

1 pound ground beef
1 tablespoon minced garlic
2 tablespoons steak sauce
Salt and pepper
¼ cup water
¼ cup finely minced onion
½ cup barbecue sauce

Combine beef, garlic, steak sauce, salt and pepper and form into patties. Cook in a skillet until just about done. Depending on amount of fat in skillet, drain excess fat leaving a bit for flavor. Return to heat and pour in water, onion and barbecue sauce. Cook burgers in sauce until excess cooks off. Serve glazed burgers hot on buns.

Stuffed Onion Cheese Burgers

1½ pounds ground beef
1 teaspoon garlic
2 tablespoons meat marinade
1 teaspoon parsley
Several slices cheese
Several slices thin-sliced onions

Combine beef, garlic, marinade and parsley; repeat until all patties are used. Make equal amounts of very thin, but wide, hamburger patties. Place a slice of cheese on one patty making sure it does not overlap edges by breaking off any overhanging bits and layering it on top. Add a few onion slices. Place another patty over and press edges together firmly. Chill to set the shape. Cook until juices run clear. Other stuffings can include everything from salsa to mushrooms.

Skillet Spaghetti & Meatballs

1½ pounds ground beef
2 medium onions, minced
1 cup crushed seasoned croutons
1 egg, beaten
Olive oil
Parmesan cheese
1 (7-ounce) package spaghetti
1 can diced tomatoes, undrained

¾ cup chopped bell pepper
⅔ cup water
1 (8-ounce) can sliced mushrooms
1 teaspoon chili powder
1 teaspoon dried oregano
1 teaspoon sugar
1 teaspoon salt
1 cup shredded Cheddar cheese

In a large bowl, combine beef, onions, croutons and egg. Roll into balls and brown in a large skillet (with lid) in olive oil and dashes of Parmesan cheese. Drain excess fat. Stir in uncooked spaghetti and remaining ingredients (drain mushrooms) except cheese. Cover and simmer until noodles are tender. Top with cheese and serve hot.

Homemade Sloppy Joe

2 pounds ground beef
4 medium green bell peppers,
    chopped (3 cups)
2 medium red bell peppers,
    chopped (1½ cups)
4 medium onions, chopped (2 cups)
1 cup prepared coffee
½ cup cider vinegar

2 cans tomato paste
½ cup water
2 teaspoons chili powder
2 teaspoons paprika
½ teaspoon salt
½ teaspoon ground black pepper
¼ teaspoon cayenne pepper

Brown meat in a large skillet; drain. In the same large skillet, combine meat and remaining ingredients. Add additional water if needed. Cook over medium-high heat until thick. Serve hot on hamburger buns.

Swiss Steak

½ pound lean bacon

3 pounds boneless beef round steak

½ teaspoon salt

½ teaspoon pepper

1 tablespoon minced garlic

6 medium-size potatoes, sliced

2 large onions, sliced

1 can sliced mushrooms, drained

1 can diced tomatoes

1 can tomato sauce

In glass baking dish, layer bacon across the bottom. Rub steak with salt, pepper and garlic; place over bacon. Layer potatoes and sprinkle with salt, pepper and garlic. Next, layer onions and mushrooms. Pour in tomatoes with juice and tomato sauce; cover and cook at 350° about 1 hour or until meat and potatoes are fork-tender.

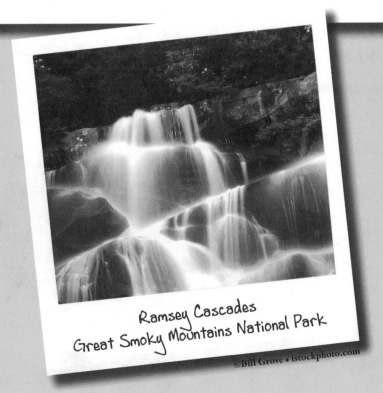

Ramsey Cascades
Great Smoky Mountains National Park

©Bill Grove • istockphoto.com

Ribeye Ale Steaks

2 (4½-inch cut) ribeye steaks
1 bottle dark ale
Black pepper
Garlic powder
3 tablespoons butter
1 teaspoon Italian seasoning
½ teaspoon lemon juice

Marinate steaks in a zip-close bag in ale about 2 hours. Remove and place on a plate or baking dish. Rub a liberal amount of black pepper and garlic powder into each steak. In a bowl combine butter, seasoning and lemon juice. Mix well and chill. Grill, bake or broil steaks to desired doneness. Let each steak rest 2 to 4 minutes before serving. Just before serving, top each steak with seasoned butter.

This recipe works with any steak but ribeyes really seem to do well.

Southern Brewers Festival
Chattanooga • August

If you like brew, this event is for you! The annual Southern Brewers Festival in early August has become one of the city's most anticipated gatherings, with good reason. During the festival, two blocks near the Riverfront are transformed into one big beer tent. Wet your whistle on more than 40 different brews as vendors from around the world serve up their best. Several local cafes are also on hand to provide a variety of culinary delights.

www.southernbrewersfest.com

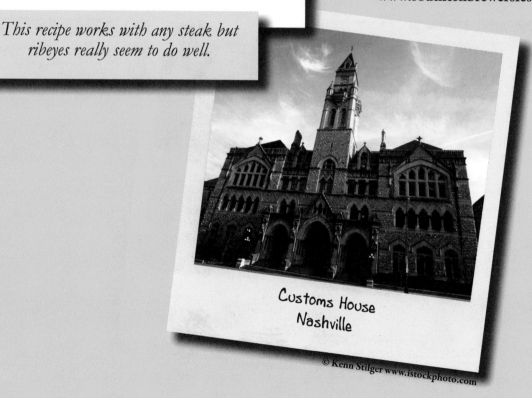

Customs House
Nashville

© Kenn Stilger www.istockphoto.com

Tennessee

Zesty Country-Fried Steak

4 chopped steaks
Steak sauce
1 egg
½ cup milk
1 teaspoon hot sauce
1 cup flour

½ cup cornmeal
½ tablespoon black pepper
½ teaspoon salt
Garlic powder
Oil
Minced onion

Brush each steak with steak sauce and set aside. In a bowl, combine egg, milk and hot sauce. Beat well. In a shallow bowl, combine flour, cornmeal, black pepper, salt, and desired amount of garlic powder. Dip each steak into egg mix then dredge in flour mix. In a skillet with hot oil, toss in onions and lay a floured steak gently into oil and onto onions. When turning the steaks for the first time, add a few more onions. Cook until golden brown. Remove from skillet and rest on paper towels before serving. Serve hot with white gravy.

London Broil

2 pounds round or flank steak
⅓ cup red wine
½ cup soy sauce
2 tablespoons brown sugar
1 small onion, minced
1 clove garlic, minced
1 teaspoon pepper
1 teaspoon Dijon mustard

Marinate meat in all of the ingredients for an hour or more. Place in a hot skillet with oil to quickly sear all sides. Place into a baking dish and cover. Bake in a 375° oven 35 to 40 minutes depending on how thick meat is. Internal temp should read 140°. Remove from oven and allow to rest a few minutes before slicing. Serve hot.

Pineapple Porterhouse & Jumbo Shrimp with Island Butter

Steaks:

2 porterhouse steaks
1 cup pineapple juice
½ cup soy sauce
Salt and pepper
Oil
Coconut (optional)

Marinate steaks in pineapple juice combined with soy sauce for 2 hours or longer in refrigerator. Remove steaks from marinade and apply black pepper and salt to each side. Cook in a skillet using a small amount of heated oil or cook on grill. While steaks are cooking, prepare Shrimp and Island Butter. When steaks are done to your liking, remove from heat and top with shrimp and butter. For an added touch top with additional coconut and place in an oven on broil for 1 minute on high rack to toast coconut.

Shrimp:

4 to 6 jumbo shrimp, de-veined and tailless
Butter
⅓ cup soy sauce
½ tablespoon ginger
2 tablespoons coconut

In a skillet over medium-high heat, combine a small amount of butter with soy sauce and ginger. When butter melts, add shrimp. Cook until shrimp are almost done; add coconut the last minute.

Island Butter:

½ stick butter, softened
¼ teaspoon sugar
¼ teaspoon liquid piña colada mix
Dash of black pepper

Combine Island Butter ingredients in a small bowl and mix. Chill before serving.

Pan-Seared New York Strips

4 New York strips
Red wine
Salt
Pepper
1 tablespoon minced garlic

Olive oil
Parsley
Dash of thyme
1 tablespoon minced onion

Baste each steak with red wine. Gently rub down with salt, pepper and garlic. Allow to rest about 10 minutes. In a skillet, heat a small amount of olive oil. Pan-sear the steaks to desired doneness; top with a dash each parsley and thyme. Remove steaks from heat and place on a serving dish to rest. While steaks rest, add a tablespoon or two of red wine to juices in the same skillet. Stir in minced onion. Mix well and allow sauce to boil. Remove from heat when sauce darkens and reduces slightly. Pour over steaks and serve.

Beef & Water Chestnut Ginger Stir Fry

1 pound sirloin steak, cut into strips
2 tablespoons flour
Oil
1 teaspoon plus 1½ tablespoons ginger
Soy sauce
2 bell peppers, cut in strips

2 cans water chestnuts, sliced and
  drained
1 onion, sliced
4 ounces snow peas
2 teaspoons minced garlic
¼ cup orange juice

Put steak and flour into a zip-close plastic bag, seal and shake until evenly coated. In a wok or skillet, heat about 2 tablespoons oil and stir in beef. Sprinkle with 1 teaspoon ginger and small dashes of soy sauce. Remove to a plate when steak is cooked. Heat about 2 more tablespoons oil; add bell pepper, water chestnuts, onions and snow peas. Add 1½ tablespoons ginger, minced garlic, orange juice and 2 tablespoons soy sauce. Stir in steak when the liquid begins to reduce in the skillet. Serve hot over rice or with noodles.

Dijon Steak and Mushrooms

4 steaks, favorite cut
3 tablespoons Dijon mustard
3 tablespoons Italian dressing
¼ teaspoon pepper
¼ teaspoon thyme
¼ teaspoon cumin
1 medium onion, halved and sliced
Large mushrooms, sliced
Worcestershire sauce
Pat of butter

In a bowl, combine mustard, Italian dressing, pepper, thyme and cumin. Marinate steaks in a zip-close bag at least several hours or overnight. Place onions and mushrooms in a bowl and dash several times with Worcestershire sauce. Grill steaks to desired doneness. While steaks are grilling, make a bowl out of aluminum foil. Place onions and mushrooms in foil with butter and brown. Before serving, top each steak with onions and mushrooms.

©Captured Nuance • istockphoto.com

A Toast to Tennessee Wine Festival
Lebanon • May

A Toast to Tennessee Wine Festival showcases great wine along with live music, gourmet food and area artisans. Several award-winning Tennessee wineries offer samples of their finest wines at the event. The festival also includes family-owned companies who either grow their own products or purchase grains and produce from Tennessee farmers for their recipes.

www.atoasttotennessee.com

Tennessee

Marinated Filet Mignon with Tomato Cream Sauce

Steaks:

4 filet mignon
Salt and pepper
Steak sauce or marinade
Red wine

Rub steaks gently with salt and pepper. Brush with steak sauce, place in a glass baking dish, and pour in red wine to cover bottom of dish. Lift steaks to allow wine to evenly coat. Cover and chill. Turn and add wine as needed. Before grilling remove from fridge and allow to rest 5 to 10 minutes to warm to room temp.

Quick Tomato Cream Sauce:

1 tablespoon olive oil
1 to 1½ tablespoons minced garlic
1 tablespoon minced onion
1 tablespoon parsley
1 teaspoon Italian seasoning
1 can diced tomatoes, undrained
2 tablespoons ketchup
⅔ cup sour cream
Milk, if needed
Salt and pepper

Heat oil in a small skillet. Add garlic, onion, parsley and Italian seasoning. Cook until lightly browned then stir in tomatoes and ketchup. Reduce liquid by ½ and stir in sour cream. Blend in a blender if desired or blend with fork. Add milk to thin if needed. Add salt and pepper as desired. Serve over grilled steaks with grilled veggies.

Italian Beef Roast

1 (2-pound) chuck roast
1 envelope dry onion soup mix
2 cloves garlic, minced
2 teaspoons freshly chopped oregano
2 teaspoons freshly chopped thyme
1 teaspoon salt
1 teaspoon freshly ground black pepper
1 medium onion, chopped

2 medium carrots, chopped
1 medium potato, chopped
1 large celery stalk, sliced
2 bay leaves
1 (6-ounce) can tomato paste
1 (16-ounce) can tomatoes, drained
  and chopped

Place roast in a glass baking dish. Combine remaining ingredients in a bowl and mix well; pour over roast. Cover with foil and bake at 350°. Check often and baste with juices as needed. When roast is almost done, slice into ¼-inch slices and layer into juices. Return to oven and continue to bake until done. Remove from oven and serve slices over angel hair or favorite pasta.

Beef and Cheese Taters

1 pound beef stew meat, finely chopped
Oil
Salt and pepper
1 small onion, sliced
1 small red bell pepper, diced
1 can mushrooms, drained
1 box cheese potatoes

Brown steak in a skillet with a small amount of oil and dashes of salt and pepper. Stir in onion, bell pepper and mushrooms. Cook over medium heat about 10 minutes. Add water, if needed. Prepare cheese potatoes in a large bowl as per box for oven cooking, but do not cook yet. Add meat mix to potatoes and pour mixture into a large, greased glass baking dish and cook, covered, in the oven as per box directions. Uncover last few minutes of cooking to brown edges, if desired.

Beef Roast

5 to 6 pound beef roast
1 cup red wine
½ cup oil
⅓ cup prepared black coffee
2 cloves garlic, minced
¼ cup minced onion

¼ cup Worcestershire sauce
1 teaspoon salt
1 teaspoon pepper
Carrots
Potatoes
Celery

Combine all ingredients except carrots, potatoes and celery and marinate 3 or 4 hours. Place in a roasting pan with some of the marinade and desired amount of chopped vegetables. Bake at 350° for 2 hours depending on thickness. Baste often.

Boiled Beef Steak Sandwich

1 (3-pound) boneless beef chuck pot roast
Oil
1 can condensed beef consommé
¾ cup water
1 package au jus mix
1 teaspoon Italian seasoning
French rolls

In a skillet, brown edges of roast in a small amount of oil. Do not completely cook, just brown edges. In a Dutch oven, combine consommé, water, mix, and Italian seasoning; add roast. Slowly bring to a boil and boil 20 minutes. Reduce heat to a simmer and cook, covered, 1 hour or until meat is tender. Shred meat with fork and serve on French rolls with juices on the side in a small dish. Skim fat from juices, if needed.

Grilled Beef Kabobs Sandwich

2 pounds thick-cut stew meat
½ cup steak sauce
½ cup Italian dressing
1 tablespoon lemon juice
6 to 8 hotdog-size French roll buns
Cheese
Grilled peppers and onion

Marinate meat in steak sauce, dressing and lemon juice for an hour. Place onto skewers; leave a small space between pieces of meat so they cook evenly. Grill evenly on all sides. Remove meat from skewers and place equal amounts on warmed buns. Serve hot topped with cheese and grilled onions and peppers.

Oven-Roasted Beef Brisket

3 pounds beef brisket
1 tablespoon liquid smoke
¼ cup dried minced onion
1 tablespoon apple vinegar
Barbecue Sauce

Rub brisket with liquid smoke; cover with minced onion and place in roasting pan. Pour a small amount of water in bottom of pan and add vinegar. Bake in a 500° oven for 30 minutes; turn once half-way through cooking time. Baste with juices frequently. When outside of brisket is browned, reduce heat to 325° and cover tightly. Add more water and vinegar if needed. Bake about an hour longer or until meat is tender. Baste with your favorite barbecue sauce and cook another 10 minutes.

Marinated Beef with Rice and White Cheese Sauce

1½ pounds beef stew meat, small chopped
½ cup red wine
1 tablespoon minced garlic
1 tablespoon steak sauce
½ teaspoon basil
Cracked black pepper
Salt
1 package beef-flavored rice mix
⅓ cup chopped celery
⅓ cup chopped green bell pepper
⅓ cup chopped onion
½ cup milk
4 to 6 slices white American cheese
½ teaspoon cumin

In a zip-close bag, combine steak, red wine, garlic, steak sauce, basil, 1 teaspoon black pepper and ½ teaspoon salt. Close and chill for an hour. Prepare seasoned rice according to directions on box. In a large skillet, cook beef, celery, bell pepper, onion, ⅛ teaspoon salt and ⅛ teaspoon pepper until meat is browned and vegetables are tender; drain. For cheese sauce, combine ½ cup milk with white American cheese in a small saucepan. Cook on medium low until cheese melts. While sauce is beginning to thicken, add cumin powder. Serve beef over rice with cheese sauce drizzled over top or on side.

Corned Beef

4 to 5 pound beef brisket
1 pound kosher salt
4 bay leaves
3 tablespoons cracked black pepper
1 onion, finely chopped
1 tablespoon salt

Place meat in a large stockpot or covered dish. Add water to completely cover; pour in salt. Refrigerate overnight or 2 days. Remove meat and rinse with clean water. Rinse all salt from stockpot, return meat, and cover with water. Add remaining ingredients and bring to a boil. Reduce heat to medium and simmer about an hour. Remove from water, place in a glass baking dish, and rub with more pepper if desired. Bake at 350° until outside is brown. Serve hot with potatoes, cabbage and bread.

Jack Daniels Country-Style Beef Ribs

5 pounds country-style beef ribs
1 tablespoon garlic
1 tablespoon pepper
1 tablespoon salt
1 tablespoon brown sugar
½ cup chopped onion
½ cup ketchup
⅓ cup Jack Daniels

Combine everything in a covered dish or zip-close bag and place in the fridge overnight. Arrange ribs evenly in a skillet and brown edges. Pour marinade into a baking dish and add ribs. Bake at 350° until meat is tender. Serve hot.

Poultry

Black Bean Chicken & Onion Rice

2 to 3 cups cubed chicken
1 can whole kernel corn, drained
1 can black beans, drained
1 can green chilies
1 can diced tomatoes
1 small onion, diced
1 tablespoon lime juice
1 tablespoon chili powder
1 tablespoon parsley flakes
1 teaspoon dried cilantro
1 package brown rice
1 envelope onion soup mix

Combine all ingredients, except brown rice and onion soup mix, in a slow cooker and cook on high about 8 hours. Cook brown rice per directions on package adding onion soup. Serve Black Bean Chicken hot over Onion Rice.

Mustard-Barbecued Chicken Tenders

10 to 12 chicken tenders
1½ cups water
1 cup barbecue sauce
1 cup yellow mustard

In a large, deep skillet, combine chicken tenders and water. Boil chicken about 5 minutes over medium-high heat. Add barbecue sauce and mustard to skillet and gently stir to mix well. Cook chicken until water is almost cooked off and sauce becomes thick. With a fork, shred chicken in skillet. Serve hot on a bun.

Chicken Baked Taco Wraps

1½ pounds ground or cubed chicken
Olive oil
1 can diced tomatoes and green chilies
½ cup water
1 package taco seasoning
1 package soft taco shells
1 cup shredded cheese

In a skillet, brown chicken in olive oil. Add diced tomatoes and green chilies with juice and water. Stir in taco seasoning. Cook until water is almost cooked off and mixture is thick. Prepare a glass baking dish with non-stick spray. Spoon equal amounts of mixture into each soft shell and spray lightly with non-stick spray or rub with butter. Place into dish and bake at 350° about 20 minutes or until shells begin to turn golden. Top with cheese. Serve hot.

Salsa Chicken Nacho Bake

2 cups cubed chicken
Oil
1 jar medium salsa
1 can black beans, drained
1 bag plain corn tortilla chips
1 cup shredded cheese

In a deep skillet, cook chicken in a small amount of oil until done and golden. Stir in salsa and beans. In a large baking pan or glass baking dish spread an even amount of tortilla chips over bottom. Top with chicken mixture and then cheese. Bake in a 350° oven until cheese melts.

Tangy Chicken Salad Sandwich

2 cans cubed chicken, drained
2 hard-boiled eggs
½ cup diced celery
½ cup diced carrots
½ cup diced onion
4 tablespoons mayonnaise
1 tablespoon Dijon mustard
2 tablespoons sweet relish
⅓ cup chopped almonds
½ tablespoon minced garlic
1 teaspoon black pepper

Combine all ingredients and chill. Serve chilled on French bread rolls with lettuce.

Crockpot Barbecue Chicken

3 boneless skinless chicken breasts
1½ cups ketchup
⅓ cup water
3 tablespoons brown sugar
2 tablespoons minced onion
1 tablespoon Worcestershire sauce

1 tablespoon soy sauce
1 tablespoon cider vinegar
1 tablespoon yellow mustard
1 teaspoon ground red hot pepper flakes
1 large dash liquid smoke
½ teaspoon garlic powder

Combine all ingredients in a crockpot, cover and cook on high about 4 hours. When chicken is done, shred with a fork or pull apart in chunks. Some water may need to be added.

Ground Chicken Meatballs and Pasta

1 pound ground chicken (or turkey)
2 tablespoons olive oil plus more for cooking meatballs
1 cup minced onion
½ cup breadcrumbs
3 tablespoons Italian seasoning
1 egg, beaten
1 box whole wheat pasta shells
1 jar pizza sauce
1 can stewed tomatoes
Parmesan cheese

Combine ground chicken, olive oil, onion, breadcrumbs, Italian seasoning and egg. Mix well and roll into meatballs. In a skillet, brown meatballs in a small amount of oil. Cook noodles in a separate pan per directions on box. In a separate saucepan, combine pizza sauce and stewed tomatoes. Cook over medium-high heat. Drain noodles. Plate equal amounts of noodles and top with sauce. Pour a generous amount of grated Parmesan cheese into a plate. As meatballs are removed from skillet, roll each hot meatball in Parmesan cheese coating well. Place over noodles and sauce.

Memphis Skyline

©Roger Cotton • istockphoto.com

Onion Soup Chicken and Biscuits

4 to 6 boneless chicken breasts
1 package (2 envelopes) onion soup mix
1½ cups water
Large canned biscuits
Yellow mustard
Honey

In a zip-close bag, combine chicken, soup mix, and water. Marinate several hours. Grill, skillet-cook or bake chicken until done and golden brown. Serve hot on large canned biscuits cooked per directions on package. If breasts are large, cut them in half to equal amount of biscuits. Serve with a sauce of equal amounts of mustard and honey.

Chicken Cordon Bleu

4 to 6 boneless chicken breasts
4 to 6 slices ham
4 to 6 thick slices Swiss cheese
1 can cream of celery soup
1 cup breadcrumbs

Pound breasts until thin. Top each with a slice of ham and a slice of cheese. Roll and place seam-side down in a prepared shallow pan. Pour soup over all and top with breadcrumbs. Bake in 325° over 1 to 1½ hours or until sauce bubbles. Cover with foil if bread begins to burn.

Ginger Almond Chicken

4 large chicken breasts

1 egg

1 tablespoon milk

1 teaspoon basil

1 teaspoon ginger

¼ cup flour

¼ cup crushed seasoned croutons

½ teaspoon garlic salt

½ teaspoon black pepper

¾ cup sliced almonds

1 tablespoon butter, softened

½ teaspoon brown sugar

Parsley

Rinse chicken and pat dry. In a bowl, beat egg, milk, basil and ginger. Mix flour, croutons, garlic salt and pepper. Dip chicken in egg and milk mixture and then roll in flour mix. Place in glass baking dish sprayed with non-stick spray or use non-stick baking sheet. Press almonds firmly into chicken until each piece is covered. Cook at 350° until chicken is firm, juices run clear and almonds are golden. Mix butter, brown sugar and parsley in a bowl and melt in microwave. Pour over chicken pieces.

Baked Citrus Chicken Breasts

4 large chicken breasts

½ cup orange juice (with pulp)

½ cup orange marmalade

Olive oil or oil

Juice of ½ lemon

1 small onion, chopped

1 teaspoon garlic salt

½ teaspoon ginger powder

½ teaspoon nutmeg

⅓ cup chopped almonds

Marinate chicken in orange juice and marmalade for about 1 hour. Heat oil in skillet over medium-high heat; add chicken (discard marinade). Top with lemon juice and onions. Sprinkle both sides with remaining ingredients just before removing from skillet. Chicken is done when juices run clear.

Italian Stuffed Chicken Breasts with Tomato & Spinach Salad

4 boneless skinless chicken breast halves
1 cup bottled oil-vinegar dressing, divided
4 slices mozzarella cheese
1 small bunch watercress, chopped
1 tablespoon basil
1 tomato, thinly sliced or diced
½ tablespoon minced garlic
½ cup bottled oil-vinegar dressing
1 tablespoon water
1 egg
⅔ cup Italian-seasoned breadcrumbs
½ cup Parmesan cheese
4 tablespoons olive oil

Salad:
Salad tomatoes, halved
3 cups spinach leaves
Parmesan cheese
Vinaigrette dressing
Diced almonds

Pound chicken to ¼-inch thick and place in large glass baking dish. Coat chicken well with ½ cup dressing. Cover and refrigerate until other items are ready. In medium bowl, place mozzarella cheese, watercress, basil, sliced tomatoes, garlic, and ½ cup oil-vinegar dressing. Mix well and refrigerate 20 minutes to soften cheese. Remove chicken from dressing; drain. Spoon equal amounts filling onto each piece of chicken. Fold over and seal with toothpicks. In shallow dish, combine water and egg. On a plate, mix breadcrumbs and Parmesan cheese. Coat chicken with egg mixture and then coat evenly with breading mix. Fry chicken in a skillet with oil on both sides until golden brown. A fork should come out clean with ease when done. Combine salad tomatoes, spinach, Parmesan cheese, dressing and almonds in a bowl and toss to mix. Serve chicken over spinach salad.

Memphis Italian Festival

Memphis • May

A community celebration demonstrating the values of family, faith and fellowship in the Italian-American tradition. Attendees will experience, music, food, fun events, a bocce tournament, grape stomping, arts and crafts and more.

www.memphisitalianfestival.com

©Memphis Italian Festival

Poppy Seed Chicken Casserole

4 chicken breasts, cooked
1 (10¾-ounce) can cream of chicken soup
1 (8-ounce) carton sour cream
⅓ cup finely chopped mushrooms
⅓ cup finely chopped spinach
2 cups crushed Ritz crackers
2 tablespoons poppy seeds
1 stick margarine, melted

Hand-shred chicken in a bowl. Add in soup, sour cream, mushrooms and spinach; stir well. Spread in 2-quart casserole dish. Combine crackers and poppy seeds with melted margarine, and sprinkle over chicken mixture. Bake at 325° 25 minutes or until bubbly.

Spicy Chicken with Pineapple Salsa

4 to 6 bone-in chicken breasts
2 tablespoons hot sauce
½ teaspoon cinnamon
Reserved pineapple juice from Pineapple Salsa recipe
2 teaspoons prepared jerk seasoning or Cajun seasoning
1 small onion, minced
Garlic powder

Pineapple Salsa:
1 can pineapple chunks (save liquid)
¼ cup minced red onion
¼ cup diced green bell pepper
2 tablespoons lime juice
1½ tablespoons chopped cilantro
1 tablespoon cumin powder
Pinch of salt and pepper

Rinse chicken; pat dry. Combine hot sauce, cinnamon and pineapple juice in a zip-close bag. Add one chicken piece at a time. Turn and coat each piece evenly. Place chicken in a single layer in a baking dish. Sprinkle Cajun seasoning, minced onion and garlic powder over both sides of chicken. Bake in oven at 400° for 35 minutes, until chicken juices run clear. In a bowl, combine Pineapple Salsa ingredients; spoon over cooked chicken before serving.

Grilled Hot Chicken Thighs

8 to 10 chicken thighs
½ cup hot sauce
½ cup honey mustard
½ cup barbecue sauce

Combine all ingredients and marinate in refrigerator at least 2 hours. Grill chicken until juices run clear. Serve hot with slaw and grilled vegetables.

Zesty Baked Chicken Thighs

8 chicken thighs
1 cup lemon yogurt
3 tablespoons honey
¼ tablespoon minced onion
½ teaspoon sage
½ teaspoon thyme
½ teaspoon minced garlic
1 tablespoon parsley
1 tablespoon apple cider vinegar

Combine all ingredients in a zip-close bag and refrigerate at least 1 hour. Discard marinade; place chicken in a glass baking dish coated with non-stick spray. Bake at 350° 20 to 30 minutes. Chicken is done when juices run clear. Serve hot with rice and mixed vegetables.

Fried Chicken

Assorted chicken pieces
1 large egg
1 can evaporated milk
Black pepper
½ teaspoon sugar
⅔ cup flour

⅓ cup cornmeal
⅓ cup finely crushed Wheat Chex
½ teaspoon baking powder
Salt to taste
Onion powder to taste
Oil for frying

Combine egg, milk, 1 teaspoon black pepper and sugar in a bowl. In a separate bowl or brown paper bag, combine flour, cornmeal, cereal, baking powder, salt and onion powder. Dip each piece of chicken in egg mix then bread mix. Place on a cookie sheet covered in wax paper; refrigerate about 20 minutes. Cook chicken in hot oil (deep fried or in skillet) until golden brown and juices run clear. Serve hot. Or, if you like extra-crispy chicken, place on a wire baking sheet on a cookie sheet in the oven and cook an additional 5 to 8 minutes at 450°.

Grilled Chicken Leg Quarters

4 to 6 chicken leg quarters
½ cup berry yogurt
1½ cups water
1 teaspoon salt
Barbecue sauce

Place chicken in a 9x13-inch glass dish. Combine yogurt, water and salt; pour over chicken. Cover and chill overnight. Soaking chicken in the yogurt and water brine overnight will make it tender. Remove chicken from brine and grill over medium-high heat until juices run clear. Baste with favorite barbecue sauce before removing from grill.

Tennessee

Piña Colada Chicken Quarters

4 to 6 chicken leg quarters
1 can sliced pineapple
1 package piña colada mix
⅓ cup pineapple rum (or regular rum)
⅓ cup soy sauce
1 teaspoon ground ginger
1 clove garlic, minced
Shredded coconut

Rinse leg quarters and pat dry. Remove excess fat and skin, if desired. Drain pineapple, reserving juice; set pineapple aside. Combine pineapple juice, piña colada mix, rum, soy sauce, ginger and garlic with chicken; marinate in a glass bowl or zip-close bags at least 1 hour. Remove from fridge and allow to warm at room temperature while oven preheats. Place chicken with marinade and pineapples in a glass baking dish. Bake, uncovered, at 400° for 30 minutes. Reduce heat to 350° and bake 20 minutes. Sprinkle with shredded coconut and cook an additional 5 to 10 minutes. Serve hot.

Grilled Jerk Chicken Wings

3 pounds chicken wings and drummies
½ cup vinegar
⅓ cup hot sauce
1 cup pineapple or orange juice
½ cup orange juice
1½ tablespoons crushed red pepper
2 tablespoons brown sugar
½ tablespoon cumin
½ tablespoon minced onion
½ tablespoon minced banana pepper

Rinse chicken and place in a large glass bowl. Coat with vinegar, hot sauce, pineapple and/or orange juice; cover. Allow to marinate at least an hour. Remove chicken from marinade and coat each piece evenly with remaining ingredients. Bake at 350° until golden brown or place on grill over medium-high heat.

Oven-Roasted Turkey

1 whole turkey, thawed
2 cups warm water
½ cup coarse salt
3 tablespoons brown sugar
2 teaspoons thyme
3 teaspoons liquid smoke seasoning
1 minced onion
2 chicken bouillon cubes
1 dark beer

Remove giblets from turkey. Rinse turkey inside and out; pat dry. In a container large enough to hold turkey plus water to cover, combine all ingredients (except turkey); add turkey and water to cover. Seal or cover and refrigerate for a day or overnight. Preheat oven to 425°. Remove turkey from brine and pat dry. Place on rack in large roasting pan. Pour 1 cup brine and ½ cup water into pan. Discard remaining brine. Bake 45 minutes. Check liquid; if necessary, add additional water to prevent pan from cooking dry. Roast 45 minutes longer then reduce oven temperature to 375° and continue to cook 30 to 45 minutes longer or until thermometer in thigh meat registers 180°. Cover with foil if turkeys gets too brown. Serve with cornbread dressing and cranberry sauce.

Left-Over Almond Turkey Stir Fry

1 pound left-over turkey
½ cup sliced scallions
Oil
2 bell peppers, cut in strips
1 bag frozen stir fry vegetables
1½ tablespoons minced ginger
2 teaspoons minced garlic
½ cup orange juice
1 tablespoon soy sauce
½ cup chopped almonds
Salt and pepper to taste

Stir fry turkey and scallions in about 1 tablespoon oil until scallions are cooked and turkey is slightly browned. Remove to a plate. Heat additional oil in skillet and stir in vegetables. Stir in remaining ingredients when veges are heated. When liquid begins to reduce, add turkey back in to reheat. Serve hot over rice.

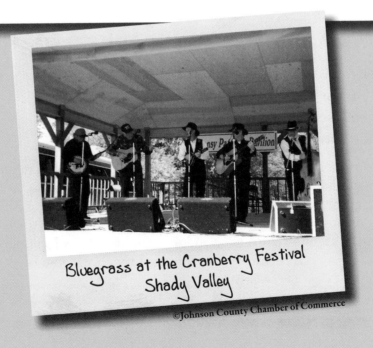

Bluegrass at the Cranberry Festival
Shady Valley
©Johnson County Chamber of Commerce

Turkey or Chicken Tetrazzini

5 tablespoons butter, divided
1 pound mushrooms, sliced
1 clove garlic, minced
¼ cup diced onion
2 tablespoons flour
2 cups water
1 chicken bouillon cube
½ teaspoon salt
¼ teaspoon pepper
1 cup cream
3 tablespoons dry white wine
2 to 3 cups cooked and shredded turkey or chicken
½ pound spaghetti, cooked
½ cup almonds, sliced
¼ cup grated Parmesan cheese

In a skillet, melt 2 tablespoons butter; sauté mushrooms, garlic and onion. In a saucepan over low heat, combine 3 tablespoons butter, flour, water, bouillon, salt and pepper; simmer. Reduce heat, and stir in cream and wine. Add chicken, cooked noodles and almonds. Place into greased baking dish. Bake at 375° about 30 minutes. Top with Parmesan cheese. Serve hot.

Italian Dressing Game Hens

6 game hens
1 bottle robust or zesty Italian dressing
1 cup crushed, seasoned croutons
1 cup freshly shredded Parmesan cheese

Clean and rinse game hens. In a large covered bowl (or several zip-close bags), marinate hens in Italian dressing in refrigerator about 2 hours. In a baking pan, evenly space the hens so they do not touch. Bake at 325° 30 to 45 minutes or until juice runs clear. Sprinkle equal amounts crushed croutons over each hen and return to oven just until brown. Remove from oven and sprinkle Parmesan cheese over each hen. Serve hot.

Fish & Seafood

Boiled Lobster

2 live whole lobsters (1 pound each)
3 tablespoons salt
3 quarts boiling water
Melted butter

Plunge lobsters head first into boiling salted water. Cover and return to boiling point. Cook 12 minutes; drain. Place lobster on its back. With a sharp knife, cut in half, lengthwise. Remove the stomach, which is just back of the head, and the intestinal vein, which runs from the stomach to the tip of the tail. Do not discard the green liver and coral roe; they are delicious. Crack claws. Serve with melted butter.

Oven Roasted Salmon with Vegetables

3 medium carrots, peeled and chopped
1 yellow bell pepper, thinly sliced
1 red bell pepper, thinly sliced
4 parsnips, peeled and chopped
8 ounces Brussels sprouts, halved
5 tablespoons olive oil, divided

⅓ cup Italian seasoning, divided
2 teaspoons salt, divided
2 teaspoons cracked pepper, divided
4 salmon steaks
2 tablespoons lemon juice

Preheat oven to 375°. Coat 2 aluminum foil-lined baking sheets with nonstick cooking spray. Arrange carrots, peppers, parsnips, and Brussels sprouts evenly on baking sheet. Drizzle with ½ of olive oil and sprinkle with ½ of Italian seasoning, ½ of salt, and ½ of pepper. Arrange salmon fillets on second sheet. Coat with remaining olive oil, Italian seasoning, salt and pepper and drizzle salmon with lemon juice. Bake the sheet with vegetables 35 to 45 minutes or until tender, stirring occasionally. Bake the sheet with salmon 15 to 20 minutes or until fish flakes with a fork. Top veggies with salmon. Serve hot.

Pan-Seared Swordfish with Lemon Yogurt Sauce

Lemon Yogurt Dipping Sauce:

1 cup plain yogurt

1 tablespoon lemon

1 teaspoon minced onion

2 teaspoons garlic powder

2 teaspoons oregano

3 teaspoons tarragon

Combine all ingredients and chill before serving with Pan-Seared Swordfish

Pan-Seared Swordfish:

4 (1-inch-thick) swordfish steaks

2 tablespoons butter, softened

2 tablespoons soy sauce

1 teaspoon garlic powder

Salt and pepper to taste

Oil

Sesame seeds

Wash swordfish steaks; pat dry. Combine butter, soy sauce, garlic powder, salt and pepper; spread over each steak evenly. In a skillet, sear both sides of meat in hot oil until golden brown. Turn as few times as possible. Steak is done when thickest part flakes with a fork. Before removing from skillet, top with sesame seeds. Drizzle Lemon Yogurt Sauce over plate and place swordfish on top.

Broiled Tuna Steaks

4 tuna steaks
Olive oil
Minced garlic
Salt
Parsley
Lime juice

Baste each steak with olive oil and rub with garlic and a dash of salt. Broil each steak 3 to 5 minutes, depending on thickness of steaks. Fish will flake with fork when done. Top each steak with a dash of parsley and a squeeze of lime juice.

Zesty Tuna Patties

2 cans tuna, drained
½ cup breadcrumbs
1 egg, beaten
⅓ cup soy sauce
⅓ cup yellow mustard
1 teaspoon pepper
1 teaspoon salt
1 teaspoon garlic powder

Combine all ingredients and form into 4 equal patties. Bake at 350° about 20 minutes or brown in a skillet with oil.

Shrimp or Scallop Hopping John

½ pound small scallops or ½ pound salad mini-shrimp
2 tablespoons olive oil
Salt and pepper
1 cup cooked long-grain rice
1 cup fresh or frozen black-eyed peas, cooked
½ cup chopped red onion
1 cup diced celery
2 tablespoons freshly chopped parsley plus additional for garnish
1 teaspoon Creole seasoning

Rinse scallops or shrimp; pat dry. In large skillet, heat oil over high heat. Add scallops or shrimp plus a dash of salt and pepper to taste. Sear scallops just until opaque or shrimp until pink. Combine scallops or shrimp with rice, black-eyed peas, onion, celery, 2 tablespoons chopped parsley, Creole seasoning and additional salt and pepper in a large bowl tossing gently. Sprinkle with parsley flakes.

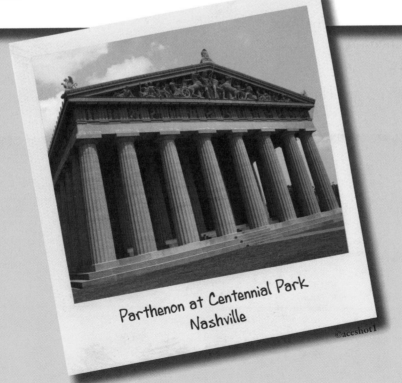

Parthenon at Centennial Park
Nashville

©aceshot1

Fried Coconut Shrimp with Piña Colada Sauce

2 pounds shrimp, shelled and de-veined
1 cup milk
1 egg
2 tablespoons pineapple juice
⅓ cup shredded coconut
3 cups flour
⅓ cup cornmeal
2 cups finely crushed tortilla chips

Combine milk, egg and pineapple juice in a bowl. In a shallow dish combine coconut, flour, cornmeal and tortilla chips. Dip shrimp in milk mixture then coat in breading mixture. Cook in hot oil until golden brown. Serve hot with Piña Colada Sauce on the side.

Piña Colada Sauce:

1 cup sour cream
⅓ cup piña colada liquid drink mix
⅓ cup shredded coconut
Dash of hot sauce

Combine all ingredients and chill before serving.

Spicy Shrimp Boil

2 to 3 pounds raw shrimp, unpeeled
1 cup hot sauce
2 tablespoons minced garlic
2 small onions, diced
2 limes, juiced
1 tablespoon salt
1 tablespoon cumin
2 teaspoons black pepper

Combine all ingredients, except shrimp, with enough water to more than cover shrimp in a large pot; boil 20 to 30 minutes. Add shrimp last 10 minutes. Serve hot with corn, potatoes and slaw.

Garlic Shrimp Pasta with a Kick

1 (12-ounce) package tri-color pasta
1 tablespoon olive oil
4 tablespoons butter
3 to 5 cloves garlic, minced
1 to 2 tablespoons Tony Chachere's (or crushed red pepper)
1 pound cooked and peeled medium shrimp
2 tomatoes, chopped
Salt and pepper to taste

Cook pasta in boiling water with olive oil until al dente; drain. Place butter and garlic in a microwave-safe bowl; microwave on high 45 seconds or until melted. Add hot seasoning; stir. In serving dish, combine pasta, shrimp, butter mixture and tomatoes; toss to combine. Salt and pepper to taste.

Country-Fried White Fish

1 pound white fish fillets (fresh or frozen)
⅓ cup yellow cornmeal
3 cups finely crushed tortilla chips
⅓ cup flour
2 teaspoons salt
2 teaspoons paprika
3 teaspoons chili powder
3 teaspoons black pepper
1 egg
3 cups milk
Oil for frying

Thaw frozen fish; dry with a paper towel. In a shallow bowl, mix cornmeal, chips, flour, salt, paprika, chili powder and black pepper. In a shallow bowl, combine egg and milk; mix well. Dip fish in milk mixture and then roll in cornmeal mixture. Fry in hot oil until deep brown and fish flakes with fork. Drain on a paper towel before serving.

World's Biggest Fish Fry

Paris • April

Start with 1,325 pounds of cornmeal, 212 pounds of salt and 10,000 pounds of fresh Kentucky Lake catfish. Add all of this with the annual Fish Fry Rodeo, the grand parade, street dances, sporting events, arts and craft shows and square dances, and you will have the World's Biggest Fish Fry.

www.worldsbiggestfishfry.com

©Brad Hosford

Broiled Catfish & Bacon Sandwich

4 to 6 catfish fillets
2 tablespoons ketchup
2 tablespoons chili sauce
4 tablespoons lemon juice, divided
¼ teaspoon hot sauce
½ teaspoon lemon pepper
¼ teaspoon salt

8 to 12 slices bacon, cooked
1 tomato, sliced
1 onion, sliced
Lettuce
Tartar sauce
Buns or bread

Preheat oven to 350°. Lay fish in prepared glass baking dish. Combine ketchup, chili sauce, 2 tablespoons lemon juice, and hot sauce. Coat fish with mixture. Drizzle remaining 2 tablespoons lemon juice over catfish; sprinkle with lemon pepper and salt. Bake until fish flakes with fork. Cook and drain bacon. Combine fish and bacon with tomatoes, onions, lettuce and tartar sauce on your favorite bun or bread.

Blackened Catfish

4 to 6 catfish fillets
Salt
1 tablespoon paprika
1 tablespoon black pepper

1 tablespoon Italian seasoning
1 tablespoon garlic powder
Butter or oil

In a glass baking dish, submerge fish in a mixture of room temperature water to cover and 2 tablespoons dissolved salt. Soak fish about 10 minutes, then rinse and submerge in clean, room temperature water. While fish soaks, mix 1 tablespoon each salt, paprika, pepper, Italian seasoning, and garlic powder in a small bowl. Place a skillet over medium-high heat to warm. Drain fish; discard water. Coat top side of fish with blackening spice. Add butter or oil to the hot skillet then place each fillet spice-side down into skillet. While cooking, quickly top the other side of the fillets with spice. Add additional butter or oil, if needed. Turn fillets and sprinkle again, if needed. Serve hot with rice when fish flakes with fork.

Catfish Amandine

2 pounds catfish fillets or nuggets
Salt and pepper
Italian seasoning
1 cup flour
Butter
Olive oil
2 cups chopped almonds
2 tablespoons chopped parsley

Pat dry fillets. Rub with salt, pepper and Italian seasoning. Roll in flour coating lightly. Fry in butter and a few drops of olive oil over medium heat for 4 minutes. Turn carefully and cook until fish is brown and flakes with fork. Fry almonds until lightly browned. Add parsley and serve over cooked catfish.

Hot Cajun-Fried Pan Fish

2 pounds cleaned pan fish
Hot sauce
1 cup buttermilk
1 teaspoon hot mustard
2 teaspoons salt
2 teaspoons Cajun seasoning
2 teaspoons ground black pepper
2 cups cornmeal

Rinse fish and pat dry. Apply hot sauce to taste coating evenly using the back of a spoon. Allow sauce to soak in. Combine buttermilk, mustard, salt, Cajun seasoning and pepper in a shallow pan; mix well. Dip fish in wet mixture then roll in cornmeal. Fry in hot oil until golden brown. Serve hot.

Lemon Butter Tilapia

8 tilapia fillets
3 tablespoons fresh lemon juice
2 tablespoons butter, melted
½ tablespoon minced garlic
2 teaspoons dried parsley flakes
Black pepper to taste
Paprika

Rinse fish with warm water and pat dry. Combine lemon, butter, garlic and parsley in a small bowl. In a baking dish coated with nonstick spray, place each piece of fish and sprinkle with pepper. Spoon equal amounts of butter sauce over fish and bake 20 to 30 minutes in a preheated 350° oven or until fish turns white and flakes with fork. Top with a very small dash of paprika.

Oven-Fried Tilapia

12 pounds tilapia fillets
Olive oil
6 teaspoons bottled tartar sauce
Lemon juice
⅔ cup seasoned fine breadcrumbs
Pinch basil

Place tilapia fillets in a well-oiled baking dish. Coat each with tartar sauce, a squeeze of lemon juice and breadcrumbs. Bake at 400° 20 minutes or until tilapia flakes when tested with a fork. Serve over rice with vegetables on the side.

Apricot Glazed Trout

4 to 6 trout fillets, skinless
1 jar apricot preserves
1 tablespoon minced garlic
2 tablespoons grated orange peel
2 tablespoons rosemary
1 tablespoon basil
¼ teaspoon salt
¼ teaspoon pepper

Preheat oven to 350°. Lightly coat shallow baking dish with nonstick cooking spray. Place fillets in baking dish. In a small saucepan over medium-low heat, stir together apricot preserves, garlic, orange peel, rosemary, basil, salt, and pepper until heated and mixed well. Pour over fillets. Bake 15 to 20 minutes or until fish flakes with a fork.

Baked Buttery Herb Fish

6 to 8 skinless fish fillets
½ stick butter, melted
Oregano
Basil
Thyme
Black pepper
Garlic powder

Preheat oven to 375°. Place fillets on a baking pan coated with nonstick spray. Lightly coat each fillet with melted butter; sprinkle with spices to taste. Cook 10 minutes per inch of thickness; fish should flake when tested with a fork. Serve with a light squeeze of lemon juice.

Tennessee

Fried Perch or White Hot Fish

1 pound perch or whiting fillets
1 egg
½ cup milk
¼ cup hot sauce
⅓ cup yellow cornmeal
⅓ cup flour
½ teaspoon salt
½ teaspoon paprika
¼ teaspoon chili powder
Oil

Combine egg and milk with hot sauce. Mix cornmeal, flour, salt, paprika and chili powder. Dip fish in milk mix and roll in breading mixture. Fry in single layer in hot oil or fat in a large pan over moderate heat for 5 minutes; turn carefully. Fry second side 5 minutes longer or until fish is brown and flakes easily when tested with a fork. Drain on a paper towel.

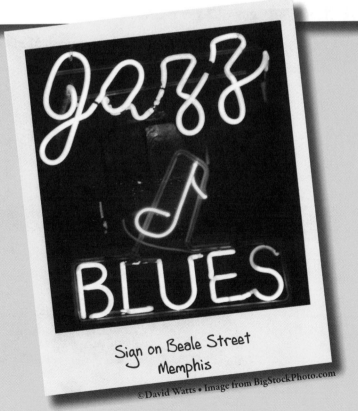

Sign on Beale Street
Memphis

©David Watts • Image from BigStockPhoto.com

Kid's Fish Tacos

1 box breaded frozen fish bites
Taco seasoning
Box hard taco shells
Salsa
Shredded cheese
Shredded lettuce

Cook fish per directions on box. Sprinkle with taco seasoning 2 to 3 minutes before removing from oven. Place in a taco shell while hot and top with salsa, cheese and lettuce and other favorite toppings. Delicious with a small bowl of applesauce on the side.

Unicoi County Apple Festival
Erwin • October

The festival, consistently named one of the Southeast Tourism Society's Top 20 Events in the Southeast and a two-year winner of a Northeast Tennessee Tourism Association's Pinnacle Award, is a premier two-day event that features handmade crafts, a variety of unique foods, two entertainment stages highlighting local, regional and national talent, large children's area, Blue-Ridge Pottery Show and Sale, Apple Festival Pageant, tennis tournament, cooking contest and much more.

www.unicoicounty.org/apple_festival.html

©Unicoi County Apple Festival

Tennessee

Blackened Grouper with Creole Mayonnaise

Creole Mayonnaise:

½ to ⅔ cups low-fat mayonnaise
1 tablespoon finely chopped shallots
½ tablespoon parsley
½ tablespoon Dijon mustard
1 teaspoon hot sauce
½ teaspoon minced garlic
Squeeze of lemon juice

Combine all mayonnaise ingredients and stir; chill before serving.

Blackened Grouper:

4 to 6 grouper fillets
2 tablespoons butter, melted
1 teaspoon olive oil
2 teaspoons paprika
1 teaspoon minced garlic
½ teaspoon black pepper
½ teaspoon cayenne pepper
½ teaspoon lemon zest

Rinse grouper fillets; pat dry and set aside. Melt butter and stir in olive oil; gently brush over fillets. Combine remaining ingredients in a small bowl; sprinkle about half over fillets. Bake at 425° or under broiler. Turn and re-coat other side; broil until golden and blackened on top. Fish should flake with fork when done. Serve with Creole Mayonnaise.

Foil-Grilled Trout

2 rainbow trout fillets
1 tablespoon olive oil
2 teaspoons garlic salt
1 teaspoon ground black pepper
1 lemon, juiced
1 lemon, sliced
1 can green chilies, drained

Rinse fish and pat dry. On large pieces of heavy-duty foil, baste each piece with olive oil. Dash with garlic salt and pepper; squeeze lemon juice over each piece. Top with lemon slices and equal amounts of green chilies. Fold foil over and pinch edges to avoid drips. Place on a medium-high covered grill and cook about 10 minutes per side. Time may vary due to thickness of fish. Serve hot when fish flakes with fork.

Pretzel-Coated Fried Cod

4 cod fillets
2 eggs, beaten
½ cup milk
Pepper
1 cup crushed pretzels
Oil

Combine eggs and milk; mix well. Dip fish into egg mixture, dash with pepper and coat with crushed pretzels. Fry in hot oil until fish flakes with fork. Serve hot.

Tennessee

Baked Almond Flounder

2 to 4 flounder fillets
2 tablespoons teriyaki sauce
2 tablespoons lemon juice
3 tablespoons butter
Minced garlic
½ cup slivered almonds

In a prepared baking dish, lay the fillets out and top with sauce and lemon juice. Bake at 400° about 15 minutes. In a skillet, melt butter and brown garlic. Stir in almonds and cook for a few minutes. Spoon mixture onto fish before removing from oven.

Tennessee Aquarium Chattanooga

©Sterling Stevens • istockphoto.com

Tequila Grilled or Seared Fish

4 to 6 favorite fish fillets
½ cup tequila
½ cup orange juice
1 small red bell pepper, sliced
Parsley
½ cup diced onion
Salt and pepper

Marinate fish in tequila and orange juice at least 2 hours or overnight. Remove from marinade and cook over a hot grill turning as few times as possible. Grill with sliced red peppers and top with parsley and diced onion. Sprinkle with salt and pepper. Serve hot. If searing, prepare fish in the same way, but use a small amount of butter and olive oil in a hot skillet. When cooking, add in peppers and onions.

Cookies & Candies

Cow Patty Cookies

1 cup shortening
1 cup butter, softened
2 cups sugar
2 cups brown sugar
4 eggs, beaten
4 cups all-purpose flour
2 teaspoons vanilla extract
2 cups quick oats
2 cups coconut
1 (12-ounce) package chocolate chips
2 cups chopped pecans
2 cups cornflakes

Combine all ingredients in a very large bowl. Drop by teaspoonful onto a prepared cookie sheet. Bake at 325° about 15 minutes.

Sweet Black Walnut Cookies

2 cups brown sugar
4 eggs, beaten
⅔ cup flour
½ teaspoon salt
½ teaspoon baking powder
2 cups chopped black walnuts

Preheat oven to 350°. Combine brown sugar, eggs, flour, salt and baking powder. Stir in chopped nuts. Drop by teaspoonful on greased baking sheet, and bake about 12 minutes.

Pistachio Chocolate Chip Cookies

3¼ cups sifted all-purpose flour
2 teaspoons baking powder
¾ teaspoon salt
1 cup butter, softened
1 cup sugar
2 eggs
2 tablespoons milk
1 teaspoon vanilla
1 package instant pistachio pudding mix
1 cup semisweet chocolate chips
1 cup chopped walnuts

Sift flour, baking powder and salt. Cream butter, sugar, eggs, milk and vanilla. Add flour mixture until blended and stir in pudding mix, chocolate chips and nuts. Shape by rounded teaspoonfuls into balls on sheet, about 2 inches apart. Flatten dough with dampened bottom of drinking glass. Bake 8 to 10 minutes or until set.

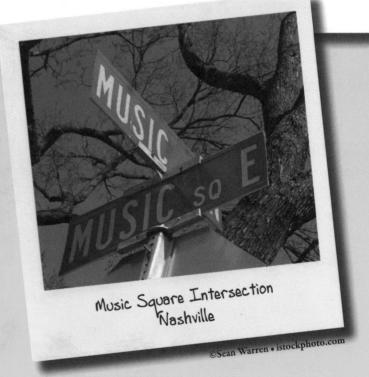

Music Square Intersection
Nashville

©Sean Warren • istockphoto.com

Country-Style Honey Cookies

⅔ cup butter, softened
1 cup honey
1 egg, beaten
¼ cup light molasses
1¾ cups whole-wheat flour
1 teaspoon salt
1 teaspoon baking soda
1 teaspoon ground cinnamon
1 teaspoon ground ginger
1 teaspoon ground cloves

Cream butter and honey. Add egg and molasses; beat well. Add flour, salt, baking soda and spices; mix thoroughly. Drop by the teaspoonful onto a greased cookie sheet, and then flatten with the bottom of glass that has been dampened with water. Brush with honey, if desired, before cooking. Bake at 350° about 10 minutes.

Music & Molasses Festival

Tennessee Agricultural Museum, Nashville • Third weekend in October

The annual Music & Molasses Festival is a country celebration of the harvest season. Molasses-making the old-time way is one of the many special demonstrations that can be enjoyed with cooking and tasting at the sorghum mill. The weekend of family fun includes bluegrass music, story-tellers, country cloggers, a grist mill, and homemade cakes and pies.

http://tnagmuseum.org/special.html

©Tennessee Agricultural Museum

Tennessee

Sugar Cookies

2½ cups all-purpose flour
1½ teaspoons baking soda
1 cup butter, softened
1¾ cups sugar, divided
¼ cup brown sugar
1 egg
1 teaspoon vanilla extract
½ cup milk

Preheat oven to 350°. In a bowl, combine flour and baking soda; set aside. In a separate bowl, cream together butter, 1¼ cups sugar and ¼ cup brown sugar. Beat in egg and vanilla; add milk. When mixed well, combine with dry ingredients. Roll dough into ping-pong size balls and roll in remaining sugar. Place cookies 2 inches apart onto ungreased cookie sheets. Bake 9 to 10 minutes for softer cookies or 10 to 15 minutes for crunchier cookies.

©Tennessee Agricultural Museum

Gingersnaps

1 cup sugar plus more for coating
2 cups all-purpose flour
½ teaspoon salt
1 teaspoon baking soda
1 teaspoon ground cinnamon
1 teaspoon ginger
½ teaspoon cloves
¾ cup shortening
¼ cup molasses
1 egg, slightly beaten

Combine 1 cup sugar with flour, salt, baking soda, cinnamon, ginger, and cloves. Cut in shortening until it resembles coarse crumbs. Stir in molasses and egg. Shape dough into 1-inch balls and roll in sugar. Place on ungreased cookie sheet and flatten slightly. Bake in preheated 350° oven about 10 minutes.

Morton's Overlook
Great Smoky Mountains National Park

© Michael Hare

Tennessee

Tennessee Tea Cake Mini Muffins

1 stick butter
1½ cups firmly packed dark brown sugar
2 eggs, beaten
1½ teaspoons vanilla
1 teaspoon almond extract
½ tablespoon orange juice
1½ cups all-purpose flour
¼ teaspoon salt
Powdered sugar

Melt butter in a medium saucepan over medium heat; add brown sugar and stir until dissolved. Set the pan aside to cool. Stir in eggs, vanilla, almond extract and orange juice. Combine with flour and salt, stirring to blend. Spoon the batter into mini muffin cups and bake at 350° about 15 minutes. While warm, coat with powdered sugar. Cakes should be a bit moist, not dry.

Pecan Pie Tea Cakes

1½ cups packed light brown sugar
1 cup all-purpose flour
½ teaspoon baking powder
1 cup chopped pecans
⅔ cup butter, softened
2 eggs, beaten
Melted butter
Powdered sugar

In a medium bowl, stir together brown sugar, flour, baking powder and pecans. Beat in butter and eggs until smooth. Spoon batter into prepared mini muffin cups. Bake at 350° for 20 minutes. Top with melted butter and powdered sugar.

Pineapple Tea Cakes

2 cups all-purpose flour
2 teaspoons baking powder
½ teaspoon baking soda
1 package vanilla instant pudding mix
⅔ cup brown sugar
1 egg, beaten
1 cup sour cream
1 can crushed pineapple in juice
½ cup oil

Combine all ingredients in a large bowl. Spoon into mini muffin cups. Bake at 350° for 20 minutes.

Union Station
Nashville

Caramel Cereal Bars

3 cups Rice Krispies
2 cups cornflakes
1 cup peanuts
1 (14-ounce) package caramels
2 tablespoons water

Lightly grease a 9x13-inch pan. In large bowl, combine cereals and peanuts. In microwave-safe bowl, combine caramels and water. Microwave on medium 3 to 5 minutes or until caramels are melted. Pour over cereal mixture and mix well. Press into greased pan. Chill 1 hour or until firm. Cut into bars.

Tangy Lemon Bars

1 cup margarine, softened
2 cups all-purpose flour
½ cup powdered sugar
¼ teaspoon salt

Combine and mix well. When soft and pliable, press into a 10x14-inch pan. Bake 20 minutes at 325°.

Topping:
2 cups sugar
4 tablespoons flour
4 eggs, beaten
4 tablespoons lemon juice
½ lemon rind, grated
Powdered sugar

Combine sugar, flour and eggs; mix well. Stir in lemon juice and grated rind. Pour over crust. Bake at 325° for 25 minutes. Sprinkle with powdered sugar. Cool, and cut into bars.

Frosted Butterscotch Tea Cookies

2½ cups all-purpose flour
½ teaspoon salt
1 teaspoon baking soda
½ teaspoon baking powder
1½ cups packed brown sugar
½ cup shortening
2 large eggs
1 teaspoon vanilla
1 (8-ounce) carton dairy sour cream
⅔ cup chopped walnuts

Combine flour, salt, baking soda, and baking powder in a bowl. In large separate bowl, beat brown sugar and shortening with an electric mixer on medium. Add eggs and vanilla; beat until mixed. Add flour mixture, sour cream and nuts. Mix well and drop rounded teaspoon-size balls of dough about 2 inches apart onto prepared cookie sheets. Bake at 350° 10 to 12 minutes or until edges are lightly browned. Frost when cooled.

Frosting:

½ cup butter
3½ cups sifted powdered sugar
5 teaspoons hot water
1½ teaspoons vanilla
⅓ cup chopped walnuts (optional)

In a saucepan, melt butter over medium-low heat; remove from heat. Stir in powdered sugar, water, and vanilla. Beat until frosting is easy to spread; stir in nuts if desired. Immediately spread on cooled cookies.

Buttermilk Brownies

2 cups sugar
2¼ cups all-purpose flour
5 tablespoons cocoa
1 cup cold water
½ cup margarine

½ cup oil
½ cup buttermilk
1 teaspoon baking soda
2 eggs
1 teaspoon vanilla

Sift sugar, flour and cocoa in bowl. In saucepan, bring to boil, water, margarine and oil. Stir in dry ingredients and mix until creamy. Add buttermilk, baking soda, eggs and vanilla; beat well. Bake at 350° in prepared pan. Cool and frost with Chocolate Butter Icing.

Chocolate Butter Icing:

1 cup sugar
6 tablespoons butter
6 tablespoons milk
½ cup chocolate chips
⅓ cup chopped nuts

Combine sugar, butter and milk in a nonstick saucepan. Bring to a full rolling boil then remove from heat. Add chocolate chips and nuts. Stir and spread on brownies.

Chocolate Bark

1 package semi-sweet baking chocolate, chopped
1 package white baking chocolate, chopped
1 cup chopped almonds, divided
½ cup chopped dried apricots, divided

Place semi-sweet chocolate and white chocolate in separate microwave-safe bowls and melt as directed on package. Add half the almonds and half the apricots to each chocolate; stir until well blended. Drop spoonfuls of the chocolate mixtures onto wax paper-covered baking sheet. Let drops touch. Alternate the colors of the chocolates. Smooth chocolate out and swirl through the chocolate mixtures with knife or spoon several times for marble effect. Chill until firm. Break into pieces.

Caramel Pecans

1½ cups sugar
½ cup packed brown sugar
½ cup canned milk
Pinch of salt
1 tablespoon vanilla
1 cup chopped pecans

Combine sugars, milk, and salt in heavy boiler over medium-high heat. Stirring continuously, bring mixture to a rolling boil then cook an additional five minutes (no more; no less). Remove from heat. Add vanilla and pecans; mix well. Pour on greased platter; cool. Break apart to serve.

Chocolate Fantasy, Chocolate Tastings
Manchester • March

What if you could actually live your chocolate fantasy with fountains of chocolate cascading down and around a mountain of fresh fruit? Giant bunnies would greet you with a hug and a handful of candy. There would be chocolate at every turn... chocolate ice cream, chocolate cheesecake, homemade fudge, pies, cakes and cookies all drenched in decadent chocolate. Think you're dreaming? You're not. It's a real Chocolate Fantasy sponsored by Fantasy Radio and featuring confectioners, caterers and chocolatiers from all over the southeast. Attendees enjoy samples of chocolate favorites and new creations, too.

©Fantasy Radio

Pralines

3 cups sugar
3½ cups pecan halves
1⅓ cups buttermilk
6 tablespoons unsalted butter
¼ teaspoon salt
1 teaspoon vanilla extract
½ teaspoon almond extract
1½ teaspoons baking soda

Line 2 baking sheets with waxed paper. In a large, heavy saucepan over low heat, combine sugar, pecan halves, buttermilk, butter and salt. Cook, stirring occasionally, until sugar dissolves completely, about 10 minutes. Do not allow mixture to boil before sugar dissolves or it may crystallize and become grainy. Increase the heat to medium-high and bring to a boil, stirring occasionally but being careful not to scrape any hardened candy mixture from the sides of the saucepan. Cook to soft-ball stage, (236° to 239° on a candy thermometer), about 15 minutes. Remove pan from heat. Stir in vanilla and almond extracts and baking soda. As soon as you add the baking soda, the mixture will become lighter in color and foamy in texture. Beat rapidly with a wooden spoon until mixture begins to cool, thicken and lose some of its shine, 5 to 7 minutes. Working quickly, drop the candy by heaping tablespoonfuls, using one spoon to scoop and another to push the mixture onto the prepared baking sheets. Let stand at room temperature until firm, about 1 hour. Eat immediately or store between layers of waxed paper in an airtight container for up to 10 days.

Red Velvet Bon Bons

**1 box red velvet cake mix
   (plus ingredients to prepare as directed)
1 (16-ounce) container cream cheese icing
1 pound almond bark (white)**

Well worth the effort!

Bake cake in a 9x13-inch pan according to directions on package; cool. Crumble into a bowl and mix in icing. Form into 1-inch balls and place on cookie sheet. Refrigerate until firm. Melt almond bark over hot water until smooth or microwave 45 seconds then at 20 second intervals until completely melted. Dip bon bons into white chocolate and place on wax paper to dry.

Peanut Butter Logs

**½ loaf sandwich bread
½ cup smooth peanut butter
½ cup butter-flavored shortening**

Cut crust from bread then cut white part into 3 strips. Put crust on a cookie sheet and bake 60 to 90 minutes at 225° until brown and crisp. While crust strips are baking, bake white bread strips just until dried out (do not brown). Crush browned crust in blender to create fine crumbs. Combine peanut butter and shortening in small saucepan. Heat until melted and stir until fully blended; remove from heat. Dip white bread strips in peanut butter mixture then roll in crumbs. Place on waxed paper to dry.

Cakes

Layered Coconut Sour Cream Cake

1 white cake mix plus ingredients to prepare per directions
2 cups sugar
1 (16-ounce) carton sour cream
12 ounces coconut
12 ounces Cool Whip

Make 2 (8-inch) cake layers using package directions. When completely cool, split each layer to create four layers. Combine sugar and sour cream; add coconut and mix well. Reserve one cup sour cream mixture and spread the rest (in thirds) between the cake layers. Combine reserved sour cream mixture with Cool Whip and frost cake. May be served immediately, but I highly recommend placing in an airtight container and refrigerating 3 days before serving.

Note: If you have only a yellow cake mix, that will work also. At Christmas, I take ½ cup coconut and add red food coloring to half and green food coloring to half and sprinkle both over the top of the cake for a delightfully festive look.

Easy Red Velvet Cake

1 package white cake mix plus ingredients to prepare per directions
½ cup buttermilk
1 package cook-and-serve chocolate pudding mix
1 tablespoon red food coloring

Butter Nut Frosting:
1 can vanilla frosting
1 tablespoon melted butter
¼ cup chopped pecans

Prepare cake according to package directions substituting half of the water with buttermilk. Stir in pudding mix and food coloring. Pour into cake pans and bake according to package directions. Combine frosting ingredients and mix well. Spread over cooled cake.

Red Velvet Cake

½ cup shortening
1½ cups sugar
2 eggs
2 tablespoons cocoa
1½ ounces red food coloring
1 teaspoon salt
2½ cups all-purpose flour
1 teaspoon vanilla
1 cup buttermilk
1 teaspoon baking soda
1 tablespoon vinegar

Cream shortening and sugar. Add eggs one at a time beating well after each. Add cocoa, food coloring, salt, flour, vanilla and buttermilk one at a time beating well after each addition. Stir in baking soda and vinegar; mix well. Pour into 2 prepared 9-inch pans and bake at 350° about 30 minutes or until a toothpick inserted in center comes out clean. Cool.

Frosting:

1 cup milk
¼ cup all-purpose flour
1¼ cups sugar
¾ cup shortening
1 teaspoon vanilla
½ cup chopped nuts

In a saucepan, combine milk and flour. Cook, stirring constantly, until thick; remove from heat. In a bowl, cream sugar and shortening until light and fluffy. Stir in vanilla and cooled cream sauce. Beat until icing becomes stiff. Add chopped nuts if desired and spread over cooled cake.

Old-Fashioned Strawberry Shortcake

2½ cups Bisquick (biscuit mix)
3 tablespoons sugar
3 tablespoons butter, melted
½ cup milk
1 (24-ounce) container sliced strawberries with sugar
3 tablespoons powdered sugar
1 (8-ounce) carton Cool Whip

Combine Bisquick, sugar, butter and milk into a dough; gently knead into a smooth ball. Pat into a disk about 8 inches in diameter and place on a sprayed baking sheet. Bake 15 to 20 minutes at 425°. Cool; cut in half horizontally. Place the bottom half, cut-side up on serving dish. Sprinkle top with juice from strawberries. Top with ⅔ of the strawberry slices. Add powdered sugar to Cool Whip in the carton and mix well; spread ½ over strawberries. Place the top layer of the cake, cut-side down, over Cool Whip. Arrange remaining ⅓ strawberries and ½ Cool Whip on top. Refrigerate until ready to serve. Serves 6 to 8.

Note: If strawberries are in season, use 2 pints fresh strawberries instead of the 24-ounce container. Wash, cap, and slice the strawberries then sprinkle with ½ cup sugar and refrigerate overnight.

West Tennessee Strawberry Festival
Humbolt • May

Strawberries of the region have been celebrated each year in May since 1936. Festivities include a recipe contest, pet parade, checker tournament, barbecue contest, 5k and 10k runs, and parades for all ages.

www.wtsf.org

Chocolate Chocolate Cream Cake

8 squares unsweetened chocolate

2¼ cups sifted all-purpose flour

2 teaspoons baking soda

½ teaspoon salt

½ cup margarine, softened

2¼ cups packed light brown sugar

3 eggs

2½ teaspoons vanilla, divided

1 cup sour cream

1 cup boiling water

⅔ cup powdered sugar

1 pint heavy cream

½ cup unsweetened cocoa powder

Melt chocolate in a double boiler (or in a small glass bowl over hot water or in the microwave); cool. Preheat oven to 350°. Sift together flour, baking soda and salt; set aside. Beat butter, sugar, and eggs at high speed until light and fluffy. Beat in 1½ teaspoons vanilla and cooled chocolate. Stir in dry ingredients and sour cream a little at a time mixing on low speed until smooth. Stir in water to make a thin batter. Pour into 2 prepared 9-inch cake pans. Bake 35 minutes or until center springs back when lightly pressed with fingertips. Split each layer in half horizontally to make four layers. Whip powdered sugar, cream, cocoa, and 1 teaspoon vanilla until stiff. Spread between layers and over cake.

Chattanooga Fudge Cake

2 cups all-purpose flour
1⅓ cups sugar
4 tablespoons cocoa
1¼ teaspoons baking soda
⅔ cup mayonnaise
1 cup cold water
1 teaspoon vanilla
½ teaspoon salt

Sift together flour, sugar, cocoa and soda. Add mayonnaise, water, vanilla and salt. Beat well and pour into Bundt pan. Bake in 350° oven until done.

Nedra's Chocolate Heaven Cake

1 German chocolate cake mix
1 package instant chocolate pudding mix
1 cup sour cream
½ cup warm water
⅓ cup vegetable oil
5 large eggs
½ cup cherries, chopped

½ cup white chocolate chips
½ cup semi-sweet mini chocolate chips
½ cup peanut butter chips
½ cup chopped pecans
¾ cup coconut
Powdered sugar (optional)

Mix cake mix, dry pudding mix, sour cream, water, oil, and eggs with electric mixer 2 to 3 minutes, until well blended. Add cherries, chips, pecans and coconut. Mix 1 to 2 more minutes. Spray tube or Bundt pan; pour in mixture. Cook at 350° 50 to 60 minutes or until toothpick inserted in center comes out clean. Cool ten minutes; remove from pan. Dust top with powdered sugar if desired. If this is not rich enough for you, it can be served with Cool Whip or ice cream. Keep tightly covered if any is left.

Pound Cake

2 sticks butter, softened
3 cups sugar
6 large eggs, beaten
3 cups self-rising flour
1 cup milk
3 teaspoons lemon flavoring
1 teaspoon almond flavoring

Grease and flour a tube pan. In a large bowl, cream butter and sugar. Add eggs one at a time beating well after each. Alternate adding flour and milk a little at a time mixing well. Stir in lemon and almond flavorings. Pour into pan and bake at 325° for 1 hour. Cake is done when a toothpick inserted in the middle comes out clean.

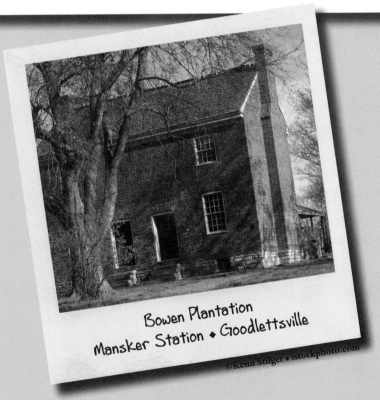

Bowen Plantation
Mansker Station • Goodlettsville

©Kenn Stilger • istockphoto.com

Caramel Pound Cake

2 sticks margarine, softened
½ cup butter-flavored shortening
1 (16-ounce) box light brown sugar
1 cup sugar
5 eggs
3 cups all-purpose flour
½ teaspoon baking powder
1 cup milk
1 teaspoon vanilla flavoring

Preheat oven to 350°. Cream butter, shortening, and both sugars. Add eggs one at a time, beating well after each. Mix flour and baking powder in a separate bowl. Alternate adding flour and milk beating well after each addition. Add vanilla and continue beating for another minute or two. Pour into a greased and floured tube pan. Bake 1 hour and 15 minutes.

Caramel Glaze:

1 cup light brown sugar
½ cup evaporated milk
1 teaspoon vanilla
1 cup sugar
1 stick butter
1 cup chopped pecans (optional)

Combine all glaze ingredients (except nuts) in a medium saucepan. Bring to a full rolling boil and boil 1 minute. Add nuts (if desired) and pour over cake.

Carrot Cake

2 cups sugar

2 cups all-purpose flour

2 teaspoons baking soda

2 teaspoons baking powder

2 teaspoons ground cloves

2 teaspoons pumpkin pie spice

1 teaspoon nutmeg

1 teaspoon cinnamon

1 teaspoon salt

5 tablespoons orange juice

4 eggs, beaten

1½ cups oil

3 cups raw grated carrots

½ cup nuts

Combine all cake ingredients, except carrots and nuts, in a large bowl. Fold in carrots and nuts. Pour into prepared Bundt or cake pan. Bake at 325° for 1 hour. Test for doneness with toothpick. Cook additional 10 minutes if needed. Top with White Cream Cheese Frosting.

White Cream Cheese Frosting:

1 (8-ounce) package cream cheese, softened

4 tablespoons butter, softened

3 cups powdered sugar

1 teaspoon vanilla

Combine ingredients and mix on low to spreading consistency.

Glazed Spiced Rum Cake

½ cup chopped pecans
½ cup chopped walnuts
1 box yellow cake mix
1 box instant vanilla pudding

3 eggs
½ cup water
⅓ cup oil
⅓ cup spiced rum

Place pecans and walnuts in the bottom of a well-greased 12-inch Bundt cake pan. Tumble with your fingers or spoon to gently mix up. In a large bowl, combine remaining cake ingredients and pour over nuts. In a 350° oven, bake about 1 hour. Remove from oven when toothpick inserted in several places comes out clean; cool.

GLAZE:

⅓ stick butter, softened
¼ cup water
½ cup brown sugar

⅓ cup sugar
⅓ cup spiced rum

Mix all glaze ingredients together and warm in microwave until butter melts. Mix well. Remove cake from pan and coat with glaze. Brush or spoon on to let hot glaze cling to cake.

Cherry Cheesecake with Pecans

2 (8-ounce) packages cream
   cheese, softened
3 eggs, beaten
¾ cup sugar

½ tablespoon vanilla
1 graham cracker pie crust
1 can cherry pie filling
½ cup chopped pecans

Preheat oven to 325°. In a large bowl, combine cream cheese, eggs, sugar and vanilla; mix well with electric mixer. Pour into crust and bake 25 to 30 minutes. Remove from oven and chill 15 minutes or more. Top with cherry pie filling and sprinkle pecans over top. Chill before serving.

Peachy Bundt Cake

¼ cup (½ stick) margarine
½ cup light brown sugar
1 large (29-ounce) can peaches
¼ cup walnuts
1 yellow cake mix
½ cup cooking oil

3 eggs
1 small jar baby food peaches
½ teaspoon nutmeg
1 large package cook-and-serve vanilla pudding

Grease Bundt cake pan. Melt margarine with brown sugar (I do this in the microwave on HIGH for 1 minute). Add 2 tablespoons peach juice from canned peaches. Place sliced peaches in each section of Bundt pan. Sprinkle with nuts. Combine remaining ingredients (using dry vanilla pudding) and beat 3 minutes. Pour over peaches and bake at 350° for 45 to 50 minutes. Cool 2 minutes before removing from pan. Delicious served with vanilla ice cream or Cool Whip.

4 Ingredient Butterscotch Cake

1 (3-ounce) box cook-and-serve vanilla pudding
2 cups milk
1 yellow cake mix
1 (12-ounce) package butterscotch morsels

Quite possibly the easiest cake ever... and it tastes GREAT!

In a small boiler over medium-high heat, combine pudding and milk; bring to boil. Remove from heat. Add cake mix; mix well. Pour into a prepared 9x13-inch glass baking dish. Sprinkle butterscotch morsels over cake. Bake at 350° for 30 minutes or until done. Cool before serving.

Pumpkin Pie Cake

1 large can pumpkin
1 can sweetened condensed milk
3 eggs, beaten
1 cup sugar
1 teaspoon nutmeg
½ teaspoon cloves
½ teaspoon ginger
½ teaspoon salt
1 teaspoon cinnamon
1 yellow cake mix
1 cup nuts
2 sticks butter, melted

Combine pumpkin, milk, eggs, sugar and spices; pour into a 9x13-inch pan. Sprinkle cake mix then nuts over top. Pour melted butter over all and bake at 350° for 50 minutes.

Great Pumpkin Festival and Weigh-Off

Allardt • October

Pumpkin growers and locals gather to judge the largest pumpkin. The Allardt Weigh-off record breaker and state record pumpkin weighed in at 1,051 pounds. In addition to breaking records, the festival includes a recipe contest, costume competition, car show and quilt show.

www.allardtpumpkinfestival.com

©Great Pumpkin Festival

Elvis Banana Cake

1 (8-ounce) package cream cheese, softened
⅓ cup milk
1 cup sugar
½ cup butter, melted
1 cup mashed bananas
3 eggs, beaten
2¼ cups all-purpose flour
1½ teaspoons baking powder
½ teaspoon baking soda
1 cup chopped walnuts

Beat cream cheese with an electric mixer until smooth. Add milk, sugar and butter; mix until well blended. Blend in bananas and eggs. Add combined remaining cake ingredients, mixing just until moistened. Pour into prepared glass cake dish. Bake at 350° for 1 hour or until a wooden pick inserted in the center comes out clean. Cool and frost with Cream Cheese Icing.

Cream Cheese Icing:

1 (8-ounce) package cream cheese, softened
¼ cup melted butter
2 tablespoons vanilla
⅔ cup powdered sugar

Combine all ingredients. Mix with electric mixer until creamy and standing with peaks.

Applesauce Cake

2 cups all-purpose flour
½ teaspoon allspice
½ teaspoon freshly grated nutmeg
1 teaspoon cinnamon
½ teaspoon ginger
1½ cups sugar
¾ cup shortening
¾ cup water
½ cup chopped nuts
1 teaspoon baking soda
1 teaspoon baking powder
2 cups applesauce
Powdered sugar

Sift flour, allspice, nutmeg, cinnamon and ginger. Set aside. Bring sugar, shortening, water and nuts to a boil; remove from heat. Add baking soda, baking powder, flour mixture and applesauce. Pour into a prepared 9x13-inch glass baking pan and bake at 350° for 35 to 40 minutes. Cool and top with powdered sugar.

Cleveland Apple Festival

Cleveland • Second Saturday in October

The Cleveland Apple Festival is a family event that takes place on the courthouse square in downtown Cleveland. Held annually, the festival offers a juried art and craft show, live bluegrass music, food booths, horse and hay rides, entertainment, an auction, and children's activities. Children's rides are free, and there is free parking.

www.clevelandapplefestival.com

©Shelley Muttart • istockphoto.com

Dreamy Creamy Pineapple Cake

1 pineapple cake mix plus ingredients to prepare
   per directions
1 (16-ounce) can crushed pineapple, drained
1 (3-ounce) package instant French Vanilla Pudding
2 cups cold milk
1 (8-ounce) package cream cheese, softened
1 (8-ounce) carton Cool Whip

Bake cake in 9x13-inch glass dish per instructions on box (I like to use the drained pineapple juice as a portion of the liquid). When cake is cooked, remove from oven and poke holes in the top with a fork. Spread drained pineapple over cake while hot. In a medium-sized bowl, prepare pudding according to directions on box using 2 cups cold milk. Add cream cheese; mix well. Pour this mixture evenly over cake. Top with Cool Whip. Keep refrigerated.

Note: A yellow cake mix and/or plain vanilla pudding can be used in place of the pineapple cake mix and French vanilla.

Peaches & Cream Cake

1 box white cake mix plus ingredients
   to prepare per directions on box
1 can peach pie filling
½ cup brown sugar
1 can sweetened condensed milk

Combine cake mix, ingredients called for on box, peach pie filling, and brown sugar. Bake as directed in a 9x13-inch glass baking dish. When cooked, poke holes in cake and pour 1 can sweetened condensed milk over cake. Allow to soak in before cutting to serve.

Little Debbie Oatmeal Cream Cake

2 Little Debbie Oatmeal Cream Cookies
1 box chocolate cake mix plus ingredients to prepare per directions
1 can chocolate icing

On a paper towel or small plate, break Little Debbie cookies into small pieces. Prepare cake as directed on box. Mix in broken cookies. Bake as directed on box in a 9x13-inch glass baking dish. Top with chocolate icing.

Chocolate Eclair Cake with Graham Crust

4 tablespoons butter, softened, divided
1 (1-pound) package graham crackers
2 small packages instant vanilla pudding
3 cups plus 3 tablespoons cold milk, divided
1 (8-ounce) carton Cool Whip
3 tablespoons cocoa
1½ cups powdered sugar
3 tablespoons Karo (or other white corn syrup)
2 teaspoons vanilla

Using 1 tablespoon butter (or more as less as needed), butter a 9x13-inch glass baking dish. Line bottom of pan with whole crackers (do not crush). Beat pudding and 3 cups milk for 2 minutes; fold in Cool Whip. Pour ½ over crackers, then place another layer of crackers on top. Pour remaining pudding over the top, then another layer of crackers. Refrigerate 2 hours before frosting. Beat cocoa, powdered sugar, 3 tablespoons butter, 3 tablespoons milk, Karo, and vanilla until smooth. Spread over top of cake. Refrigerate overnight. Makes 14 to 16 servings.

Pies & Other Desserts

Country Sugar Cream Pie

1 cup sugar
4 tablespoons flour
¼ teaspoon salt
2½ cups half and half
2 tablespoons butter
2 teaspoons vanilla
Yellow food coloring
1 unbaked pie shell
Dash of cinnamon
Dash of nutmeg

Mix sugar, flour, salt, half and half, butter, vanilla and a few drops of food coloring in a saucepan; bring to a boil. Remove from heat and stir until smooth. Pour into pie crust and sprinkle with cinnamon and nutmeg. Bake at 425° 10 to 15 minutes. Reduce heat to 325° and bake 45 minutes more. Allow to cool before serving.

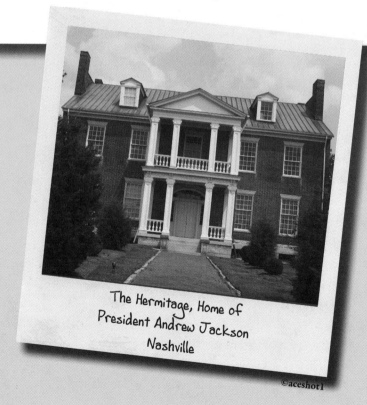

The Hermitage, Home of
President Andrew Jackson
Nashville

©aceshot1

Tennessee

Southern Pecan Pie

3 eggs
1 cup sugar
1 cup light or dark corn syrup
2 tablespoons melted butter
1 teaspoon vanilla extract
1½ cups pecans
1 unbaked, still frozen deep-dish pie crust

Beat eggs with fork in medium bowl and add in sugar, corn syrup, butter and vanilla. Mix well then stir in pecans. Pour pecan filling into pie crust and bake on a cookie sheet in a 350° oven for 55 to 60 minutes. Center should be firm. Allow to cool before cutting.

Jack Black Pecan Pie

1 (8-inch) unbaked pastry shell
4 eggs
1¼ cups brown sugar
¾ cup maple syrup
3 tablespoons melted butter
1½ tablespoons Jack Daniels
1¼ cup chopped pecans

Preheat oven to 400° and bake shell about 5 minutes. Mix eggs, sugar, syrup, butter and bourbon together; beat well. Remove shell from oven and spread pecans on shell. Slowly pour syrup mixture over pecans. Bake about 45 minutes at 350°.

Chocolate Chess Pie

1½ cups sugar
⅓ cup all-purpose flour
⅓ cup butter
2 teaspoons unsweetened cocoa powder
3 extra-large eggs
1¼ cups evaporated milk
¼ cup light corn syrup
1 ounce sweet chocolate, melted
2 teaspoons vanilla extract
1 (9-inch) unbaked pie shell or refrigerated ready-made pie crust

Preheat oven to 375°. In a large bowl, combine sugar, flour, butter and cocoa. Mix well. Add eggs one at a time, mixing well after each addition. Add evaporated milk, corn syrup, chocolate and vanilla. Mix well. If using refrigerated crust, unroll and place into pie pan. Pour batter into pie shell. Bake 45 to 50 minutes or until wooden pick inserted in center comes out almost clean.

Old-Fashioned Pineapple Pies

2 (9-inch) pie shells, unbaked
1 egg, separated
1 stick butter, softened
1½ cups sugar
3 whole eggs
2 tablespoons self-rising flour
1 (15.25-ounce) can crushed pineapple, drained

Brush pie shells with slightly beaten egg white. Set aside. Cream butter and sugar. Add remaining egg yellow and three whole eggs; beat well. Stir in flour and pineapple mixing well after each. Pour mixture into pie shells and bake at 350° for 30 to 40 minutes until almost set. The last few minutes of cook time, shake pies and remove from oven when pies are firm but still shake slightly in the middle.

Sliced Apple Pie

3 pounds apples, thinly sliced
¾ cup sugar
½ teaspoon cinnamon
½ teaspoon freshly grated nutmeg
2 tablespoons cornstarch
¼ teaspoon salt
1 tablespoon fresh lemon juice
1 tablespoon butter, melted
2 ready-to-use pie crusts
1 tablespoon brown sugar mixed with 1 tablespoon melted butter

Combine apples with sugar, cinnamon, nutmeg, cornstarch, salt, lemon juice and butter. Layer apple slices in crust flat on top of each other. Cover with second crust and cut slits in top. Bake in preheated oven at 375° for 1 hour or until top crust is golden brown. Brush top crust with brown sugar mixture 5 minutes before removing from oven.

Hunka Burning Love
Peanut Butter Pie

4 ounces cream cheese, softened
1 cup powdered sugar
1 (8-ounce) carton Cool Whip
¾ cup of peanut butter
1 (9-inch) graham cracker pie crust

Mix cream cheese and powdered sugar until fluffy. Fold in Cool Whip and peanut butter. Spoon filling into crust and smooth top. Refrigerate while making Chocolate Glaze Topping.

Chocolate Glaze Topping:

2 ounces chocolate chips
¼ cup whipping cream
1 teaspoon corn syrup
4 graham crackers, crushed and chopped nuts for topping (optional)

In a small saucepan over low heat, melt chocolate chips; stir in cream and corn syrup until smooth. Remove from heat. Gently glaze over pie. Chill at least two hours before serving. Top with crushed graham crackers and chopped nuts if desired.

Quick Chocolate Pie

1 cup chocolate chips, divided
1 (8-ounce) carton Cool Whip
1 cup cold milk
1 small package instant chocolate pudding
1 graham cracker pie crust

Melt ½ cup chocolate chips in microwave; mix into Cool Whip. Beat cold milk and pudding until thick. Combine with Cool Whip mixture. Pour into pie crust and sprinkle remaining chocolate chips on top. Chill until set.

Chocolate Ice Box Pie

1 (9-inch) pie shell, half baked
1 (14-ounce) can sweetened condensed milk
4 (1-ounce) squares unsweetened chocolate
¼ teaspoon salt
½ cup water
½ teaspoon vanilla extract
Cool Whip

Cook milk, chocolate, salt and water in top of double boiler over hot water. Allow to thicken. Stir in vanilla extract. Pour into pie shell; refrigerate to set. Serve cold with Cool Whip.

Banana Cream Pie

1 small package instant vanilla
   pudding mix
1 envelope whipped topping mix
1½ cups cold milk
½ teaspoon vanilla
1 ready-made chocolate pie crust
2 medium bananas, sliced
⅓ cup vanilla wafers, crushed

Combine dry vanilla pudding mix and dry whipped topping mix with milk and vanilla with electric mixer on low speed until blended. Increase speed and blend until thick. Pour ⅓ into crust. Layer slices of banana on top, reserving ½ banana for garnish. Pour remaining filling into crust. Chill 2 hours. Garnish with sliced banana and crushed wafers.

Freezer Strawberry Pies

1 (8-ounce) package cream cheese, softened
1 cup sugar
1 teaspoon vanilla extract
4 cups chopped strawberries
1 (8-ounce) carton Cool Whip
½ cup chopped pecans
2 chocolate crumb crusts
4 to 6 graham crackers, crushed

In a large mixing bowl, beat cream cheese, sugar and vanilla until smooth. Fold in strawberries, Cool Whip and pecans. Pour into crusts. Cover and freeze 3 to 4 hours or until firm. Remove from freezer 15 to 20 minutes before serving and top with crushed graham cracker crumbs.

Pumpkin Gingersnap Pie

1½ cups cold milk
1 package instant vanilla pudding
1 (8-ounce) carton Cool Whip
1 cup gingersnap crumbs
1 cup chopped pecans
½ cup canned pumpkin pie mix
½ teaspoon vanilla extract
1 prepared graham cracker pie crust

Beat milk and pudding for 2 minutes. Stir in Cool Whip, gingersnap crumbs, pecans, pumpkin pie mix and vanilla. Mix all together and pour in pie crust. Place in the freezer at least an hour before serving. Top with additional Cool Whip and chopped nuts, if desired.

Traditional Microwaved MoonPie

1 MoonPie
1 microwave
1 scoop of ice cream
1 Double Cola

From the first time microwaves were available at gas station food stands, the microwaved MoonPie has been a Tennessee tradition. If you can muster up a scoop of ice cream and a Double Cola, you can enjoy a Tennessee MoonPie Feast!

Remove MoonPie from wrapper because this is going to get messy. Place in a small bowl or on a paper plate; microwave on high until the filling puffs up. (Be careful, the inside filling gets hot.) Top with ice cream and enjoy with a cold Double Cola.

©MoonPie

The MoonPie® was concocted in Chattanooga at the Chattanooga Bakery in the early 1900's when the reported inventor asked miners what they might enjoy as a snack. In addition to being solid and filling, the other requirement was that the size be about as big as a man's hands framing the full moon in the sky. These requirements were combined with the observation that workers at the bakery dipped graham crackers into marshmallow and laid them in the window to harden. A second graham cracker and a coat of chocolate were added to the recipe and samples were distributed to factory workers. Samples were also sent around routes with salespeople. The response was so favorable that the MoonPie became a regular item for the bakery. By the late 1950's the MoonPie had grown in popularity so much that the bakery did not have the resources to produce items other than the MoonPie.

MoonPie Vanilla Pudding

6 MoonPies
2 boxes instant vanilla pudding
Chocolate or caramel chips

Break MoonPies into smaller pieces and spread evenly over the bottom of a glass baking dish. Prepare pudding as directed on box and spread evenly over MoonPies. Chill to set pudding. Spoon equal amounts into serving bowls and sprinkle with chocolate or caramel chips.

RC and MoonPie Festival

Bell Buckle • June

Join in the cutting of the world's largest MoonPie at the RC and MoonPie Festival. Along with the food treats, there is plenty of country and bluegrass music, clogging dancers, MoonPie games, crafts, and the ever-popular "Synchronized Wading Extravaganza".

www.bellbucklechamber.com/events.html

©RC & MoonPie Festival

Goo Goo Ice Cream Stack

1 white chocolate candy bar (optional)
4 Goo Goo Cluster candy bars
4 scoops vanilla ice cream
Chocolate hard shell syrup

If desired, shave white chocolate bar and chill until ready to use for garnish. Place one Goo Goo bar onto each of four small plates or bowls. Microwave each 30 seconds on high. You want the bar to keep its shape but be warmed inside and out. Top with a scoop of ice cream then hard shell chocolate and white chocolate shavings.

After the Goo Goo Cluster® was created in Nashville in 1912 by the Standard Candy Company, it took a while to name the caramel, marshmallows, peanuts and chocolate concoction. Rumor has it that the inventor, Howard Campbell, sought naming suggestions from fellow streetcar-riders in the mornings. The rumor is that Campbell was bragging about his child's first words when a teacher riding the streetcar suggested using "goo-goo" as the baby's first words and the name of the candy bar.

Mixed Berry and Peach Cobbler

1 cup strawberries
1 cup blueberries
1 cup raspberries or blackberries
1 can peach pie filling
2 tablespoons cornstarch
¾ cup sugar
2 tablespoons plus 1 teaspoon brown sugar, divided
1½ cups self-rising flour
¼ teaspoon salt
⅓ cup plus 2 tablespoons butter, melted, divided
⅓ cup milk
¼ cup apple juice
Dash nutmeg
Dash cinnamon

Use fresh fruit if possible. Wash berries; mix with peach pie filling, cornstarch, ¾ cup sugar and 2 tablespoons brown sugar in a large bowl coating berries well.

Combine flour, salt, ⅓ cup melted butter, milk, and apple juice in another bowl; mix well. Pour berry mixture into a baking dish; spoon flour mixture over top. Bake at 375° for 25 to 30 minutes or until topping is golden brown. About 5 minutes before removing from oven, combine 2 tablespoons melted butter, nutmeg, cinnamon, and 1 teaspoon brown sugar in a small bowl and brush over top. Serve hot.

Lynnville Blackberry Festival
Lynnville • Last weekend in June

Blackberry treats and "the world's largest blueberry pie" are served at this two-day festival in south/central Tennessee. Festival attendees enjoy a street dance, live music, the Jolly Carnival featuring rides for the children, and more. This festival is "Southern hospitality at its best."

www.gilescountytourism.com

Tennessee

Easy Peach & Blueberry Dump Cobbler

16 ounces frozen peaches
½ cup frozen blueberries
1 box Jiffy yellow cake mix
1 (12-ounce) can diet cream soda
1 teaspoon cinnamon

Place peaches and blueberries evenly across bottom of a glass 9x13-inch dish. Pour cake mix over top and very gently pour diet cream soda over cake mix. Bake uncovered at 350° 30 minutes or until topping is golden brown. Sprinkle with cinnamon last 5 minutes of cook time.

RC & MoonPie Festival
Bell Buckle

©RC & MoonPie Festival

Heavenly Butterfinger Trifle

6 Butterfinger candy bars
½ cup butter, melted
2 eggs, beaten
2 cups powdered sugar
2 teaspoons vanilla
1 (8-ounce) carton Cool Whip
1 (16-ounce) angel food cake

Crush candy bars in food processor (or in zip-close bag with rolling pin); set aside. Add melted butter to beaten eggs and whisk together well. Add powdered sugar and vanilla; whisk until smooth. Fold in Cool Whip just until mixed. Break angel food cake into small pieces. Layer half the cake pieces, half the creamed mixture, and half the Butterfingers in a trifle dish (or 9x13-inch glass dish). Repeat. Cover and refrigerate overnight.

Tennessee Festivals

The following is a list of more than 200 annual festivals found throughout Tennessee. Chances are, we've negelected to include some events; if you aware of any we missed, call us toll-free 1.888.854.5954 and we'll do our best to include it in a subsequent printing. Keep in mind, too, that dates and venues change. Please verify all information before making plans to attend any of these events. Festivals are listed alphabetically by the city where the festival is held. Please call or visit the festival's website for more information. This list was compiled with the help of the Tennessee Department of Tourist Development. Go to www.TNvacation.com or call 800-GO2-TENN for more information about visiting Tennessee and to order your free Tennessee Vacation Guide.

Adamsville • Sheriff Buford Pusser Festival
May • 731-632-4080
www.sheriffbufordpusser.com

Alcoa • FreedomFest
June • 865-380-4787
www.cityofalcoa-tn.gov

Allardt • Great Pumpkin Festival & Weigh-Off
October • 931-879-9948
www.allardtpumpkinfestival.com

Ardmore • Ardmore Renaissance Faire
April • 265-423-7588
www.ardmorechamberofcommerce.com

Ardmore • Crepe Myrtle Festival
August • 931-363-3789
www.gilescountytourism.com

Ashland City • Summerfest
June • 615-792-2655
www.cheathamchamber.org

Athens • National MooFest
May • 423/745-0261
www.nationalmoofest.com

Athens • Pumpkintown Festival
October • 423-745-0334
www.pumpkintowninathens.com

Auust • The Nashville Shakespeare Festival
Nashville • 615-255-2273
www.nashvilleshakes.org

Bell Buckle • RC and Moon Pie Festival
June • 931-389-9663
www.bellbucklechamber.com/rcmoon.htm

Bell Buckle • Motorcycle Days
May • 931-389-9663
www.bellbucklemotorcycledays.com

Belvidere • Bluesfest
May • 931-967-1727
www.belvideremarket.com

Benton • Polk County Ramp Tramp Festival
April • 423-338-4503

Big Sandy • Big Sandy Spring Festival
May • www.bsspringfestival.tripod.com

Brighton • Brighton Festival
June • 901-476-8661

Brownsville • Hatchie Fall Fest
October • 731-780-5144
www.allaboutbrownsville.net/hatchiefallfest

Bruceton • Bruceton in May Festival
May • 731-586-2401

Burns • Americana Folk Festival
November • 615-446-2349
www.dicksoncountychamber.com

Byrdstown • Sierra Hull Bluegrass Festival
September • 888-406-4704
www.dalehollow.com/bg.htm

Cambden • Ryan Holladay Bluegrass Festival
September • 731-441-2214
www.ryanholladay.com

Camden • Tennessee River Pearl Festival
June • 731-584-7880
www.tennesseeriverpearlfestival.com

Carthage • Defeated Creek Bluegrass Festival
June • 615-774-3230
www.smithcountychamber.org

Caryville • Louie Bluie Music & Arts Festival
June • 423-562-8189
www.louiebluie.org

Centerville • Grinder's Switch Music & Arts Festival
September • 931-729-5774
www.hickmanco.org

Chapmansboro • Owen Farm Fall Festival
September • 615-792-7422
www.owenfarm.com

Charlotte • Promise Land Community Festival
June • 615-789-5859
www.dicksoncountychamber.com

Charlotte • Charlotte Festival
September • 615-789-4184

Chattanooga • 4 Bridges Arts Festival
April • 423-265-4282
www.4bridgesartsfestival.org

Chattanooga • Southern Brewers Festival
August • 423-757-5259
www.southernbrewersfestival.com

Chattanooga • Riverbend Festival
June • 423-756-2211
www.riverbendfestival.com

Chattanooga • Three Sisters Music Festival
October • 423-265-0771
www.downtownchattanooga.org

Chattanooga • Chattahippie Music Festival
September • www.chattahippie.com

Chattanooga • Culture Fest
September • 800-267-4232
www.artsedcouncil.org

Clarkrange • Parkfest
June • 931-879-9876

Clarksburg • Hummingbird Festival
May • 731-986-5547

Clarksville • Rivers & Spires Festival
April • 931-245-4344
www.riversandspires.com

Clarksville • International Festival
May • 931-645-6275

Clarksville • Oktoberfest
October • 931-645-3382

Clarksville • Riverfest Celebration
September • 931-645-7444
www.clarksvilleriverfest.com

Cleveland • White Oak Mountain Bluegrass Festival
July • 423.476.9310
www.whiteoakbluegrass.com

Cleveland • Cleveland Apple Festival
October • www.clevelandapplefestival.com

Cleveland • Nillie Bipper Arts & Crafts Festival
October • 423-478-3114

Clifton • Horseshoe Riverbend Festival
September • 931-676-5510
www.cliftonrotary.com

Coker Creek • Autumn Gold Festival
October • 423-261-2310
www.monroecounty.com

College Grove • Cruzin' the Grove Festival
September • 615-368-3456

Collierville • Mulberry Fest
October • 901-853-1949
www.mulberryfest.com

Collinwood • Old Timer's Day
September • 931-724-9562

Columbia • Mule Day
April • 931-381-9557
www.muleday.com

Columbia • Train Stop Storytelling Festival
May • 931-375-6103

Cookeville • Jammin at Hippie Jack's Americana Music Festival
May • 931-445-2072
www.jamminathippiejacks.com

Cookeville • Railroad Rendezvous Springfest
May • 931-526-2211

Cookeville • Holiday Festival
November • 931-372-3051
www.tntech.edu/craftcenter/holiday.html

Cookeville • Fall FunFest
September • 931-528-4612
www.fallfunfest.com

Corryton • Daylily Festival
June • 800-532-9545
www.oakesdaylilies.com

Cosby • Cosby Ramp Festival
May • 423-623-1009
www.cosbyrampfestival.org

Cottage Grove • Freedom Festival
July • 731-782-3692

Covington Glen • Tennessee Renaissance Festival
May • 615-395-9950
www.tnrenfest.com

Crossville • Crossville Depot Days
June • 931-261-7738
www.crossville-chamber.com

Crossville • Crossville Oktoberfest
October • 931-707-7291
www.crossvilleoktoberfest.com

Crossville • Homestead Apple Festival
September • 931-484-7320
www.crossville-chamber.com

Dayton • Scopes Trial Festival
July • 423-775-0361
www.rheacountyetc.com

Dayton • Tennessee Strawberry Festival
May • 423-775-0361
www.tnstrawberryfestival.com

Dayton • PumpkinFest
October • 423-775-9847
www.mainstreetdayton.org

Decatur • Fall Festival
October • 423-334-5496
www.meigscountytnchamber.org

Diana • Diana Singing
June • 931-363-3204
www.dianasinging.com

Dickson • Dickson Fiddlers Contest & Family Fun Festival
June • 615-446-5914
www.dicksoncountychamber.com

Dickson • Robert Spicer & Arthur Smith Bluegrass Festival
June • 877-718-4967
www.dicksoncountychamber.com

Dickson • Old Timers Day Festival
May • 615-446-2349
www.dicksoncountychamber.com

Dickson • Christmas in the Country Arts & Crafts Festival
November • 615-943-6275

Dresden • Tennessee Iris Festival
April • 731-364-5101
www.tennesseeirisfestival.com

Dyersburg • Juneteenth Celebration
June • 731-285-3433

Dyersburg • Main Street Fall Festival
September • 731-285-3433

Elizabethton • Sycamore Shoals Native American Festival
June • 423-543-5808
www.sycamoreshoals.org

Erwin • Unicoi County Apple Festival
October • 423-743-3000
www.unicoicounty.org/apple_festival.html

Etowah • Arts & Crafts Festival
October • 423-263-9475
www.etowahcoc.org

Eva • Beach Music Festival
May • 731-584-2128

Fayetteville • Chili Cook-off & Salsa Tasting
March • 256-533-1111

Fayetteville • Lincoln County Bluegrass & Crafts Festival
September • 931-438-9230
www.lincolncountytn.com/bluegrass

Flag Pond • Flag Pond Ramp Festival
May • 423-743-3430

Franklin • Main Street Festival
April • 615.591.8500
www.historicfranklin.com

Franklin • Celebration of Nations Festival
March • 615-794-4254 ext. 233

Franklin • Feile Franklin
March • 615-591-8500
www.historicfranklin.com

Franklin • Wine Festival
October • 615-329-9191
www.franklinwinefestival.com

Franklin • Pumpkinfest
October • 615.591.8500
www.historicfranklin.com

Gallatin • Square Fest
April • 888-301-7866
www.sumnercvb.com

Gallatin • Main Street Festival & Barbecue Cook-Off
October • 888-301-7866
www.sumnercvb.com

Gatlinburg • Festival of Christmas past
December • 865-436-1291
www.nps.gov/grsm

Gatlinburg • Craftsmen's Fair
July • 865-436-7479
www.craftsmenfair.com

Gatlinburg • Fine Arts Festival
May • 865-436-7484
www.gfaf.net

Gatlinburg • Scottish Festival & Games
May • 800-568-4748
www.gsfg.org

Gatlinburg • Festival of Trees
November • 800-568-4748
www.eventsgatlinburg.com

Gatlinburg, Pigeon Forge , Sevierville Smoky Mountain Harvest Festival
September • 888-766-5948
www.gatlinburg.com

Germantown • Germantown Festival
September • 901-757-9212

Granville • Fall Celebration Quilt & Storytelling Festival
October • 931-653-4511
www.granvillemuseum.com

Gray • "Going - Going - Green" Garden Fest
May • 423-477-3211
www.bestofshoware.com/appalachianfair

Nashville • Tomato Art Fest
August • 615-226-2070
www.tomatoartfest.com

Greenback • Strawberry Jam Festival
May • 865-856-3517
www.thecornmaze.net

Greeneville • Aussie Fall Fest Chillin' & Grillin'
October • 423-638-4111
www.greenecountypartnership.com

Gruetli-Laager • Swiss Heritage Festival
July • 423-424-4267
www.swisshistoricalsociety.org

Harriman • Polk Salad Festival
May • 865-882-8867
www.roanealliance.org

Harriman • Labor Day Festival
September • 800-FUN-IN-TN
www.roanealliance.org

Henderson • Chickasaw State Park Craft Festival
October • 731-989-5141

Hendersonville • Freedom Festival
July • 615-824-2818
www.hendersonvillechamber.com

Hendersonville • Fall Festival by the Lake
September • 615-230-8474
www.sumnercvb.com

Henry • Pioneer Days
September • 731-243-3833

Hilham • National Rolley Hole Marbles Championship & Festival
September • 800-713-5157

Rugby • Festival of British & Appalachian Culture
May • 888-214-3400
www.historicrugby.org

Hohenwald • Sonnenschein Festival
June • 931-796-4361
www.sonnenschein-tenn.org

Hohenwald • Oktober Heritage Festival
October • 931-796-4084
www.hohenwaldlewischamber.com

Holladay • Old Time Fiddler's Championship & Bluegrass Jamboree
April • 731-847-2274
www.holladaybluegrass.com

Humbolt • West Tennessee Strawberry Festival
May • 731-784-1842
www.wtsf.org

Jackson • Rockabilly Festival
August • 731-427-6262
www.rockabillyhall.org

Jackson • Shannon Street Blues & Heritage Festival
June • 731-427-7573
www.downtownjackson.com

Jackson • Celtic Fest
November • 731-697-3833
www.cswt.org

Jackson • Skyfest Tennessee
October • 731-664-3640

Jackson • African Street Festival
September • 731-267-3212
www.saaca.com

Jackson • Casey Jones Old-time Music Festival
September • 800-748-9588
www.caseyjones.com

Jefferson City • Cardboard Boat Race Festival
July • 865-262-8288
www.jcfol.com

Johnson City • Blue Plum Festival
June • 423-928-3479
www.blueplum.org

Jonesborough • QuiltFest
July • 423-753-6644
www.tennesseequilts.com/quiltfest.html

Jonesborough • National Storytelling Festival
October • 800-952-8392
www.storytellingcenter.net

Kingsport • Tomato Fest
August • 423-246-6550
www.downtownkingsport.org

Kingsport • Folklife Festival
July • 423-239-6786

Kingsport • FunFest
July • 423-392-8809
www.funfest.net

Knoxville • Knoxville Jazz Festival
April • 865-215-8729

Knoxville • Market Square Dogwood Arts Festival
April • 423-637-4561
www.dogwoodarts.com

Knoxville • Rossini Festival
April • 865-524-0795
www.rossinifestival.org

Knoxville • Festival on the Fourth
July • 865-215-4248
www.cityofknoxville.org

Knoxville • Kuumba Festival
June • 865-546-9705
www.kuumbafesttn.com

Knoxville • Boomsday Festival
September • 800-727-8045
www.boomsday.org

Knoxville • Greek Fest
September • 865-522-5043
www.greekfesttn.com

Knoxville • Pellissippi State
Hot Air Balloon Festival
September • 865-694-6528

La Vergne • Old Timers' Day
September • 615-287-8690
www.lavergne.org

Lawrenceburg • David Crockett Days
August • 931-762-9408

Lawrenceburg • Libertyfest
July • 931-762-7617
www.cityoflawrenceburgtn.com

Lebanon • Oktoberfest
October • 615-443-6635

Lenoir City • Rockin' the Docks
July • 865-986-1223
www.lenoircitygov.com

Lenoir City • Arts & Crafts Festival
June • 888-568-3662
www.lcsuburbia.org

Lenoir City • Tennessee State
Bar-B-Q & Fall Festival
October • 865-389-6106
www.tennesseestatebbq.com

Lewisburg • Goats Music
and More Festival
October • 931-359-1544
www.goatsmusicandmore.com

Lexington • Henderson
County Folk Festival
May • 731-968-3239
www.everetthornlibrary.org

Lookout Mountain • Ketner's Mill
Country Arts Fair
October • 423-821-3238
www.ketnersmill.org

Lookout Mountain • Rocktoberfest
October • 706-820-2531
www.seerockcity.com/rocktoberfest

Lynchburg • Frontier Days
June • 931-433-8461
www.lynchburgtenn.com

Lynnville • Blackberry Festival
June • www.gilescountytourism.com

Lynnville • Summer Celebration
June • 931-527-3158
www.lynnvillerailroadmuseum.com

Madison • Bluegrass Music
Festival and Contest
June • 615-945-0656
www.larrysgrandolegarage.com

Manchester • Bonnaroo
Music & Arts Festival
June • 931-728-7635
www.bonnaroo.com

Manchester • Christmas
Arts & Crafts Festival
November • 931-728-0509

Manchester • Manchester-Coffee
County Wine Festival
November • 931-728-7635
www.macoc.org

Manchester • Old Timer's Day
October • 931-728-0273
www.macoc.org

Martin • Tennessee Soybean Festival
September • www.tnsoybeanfestival.org

Maryville • Foothills Fall Festival
October • 865-273-3445
www.foothillsfallfestival.com

Maryville • Festival 4 Fun
September • 865-380-5370
www.joshuaresourcecenter.org

Memphis • Africa in April
Cultural Awareness Festival
April • 901-947-2133
www.africainapril.org

Memphis • Music & Heritage Festival
August • 901-525-3655
www.southernfolklore.com

Memphis • Beale Street
Zydeco Festival
February • 901-619-5865
www.southernculturalalliance.com

Memphis • Memphis in May
International Festival
May • 901-525-4611
www.memphisinmay.org

Memphis • Memphis Italian Festival
May • 901-685-1378
www.memphisitalianfestival.com

Memphis • Our Big Fat Greek Festival
May • 901-327-8177
www.memphisgreekfestival.com

Memphis • Enchanted Forest
Festival of Trees
November • 901.525.TREE
www.theenchantedforest.org

Memphis • River Arts Festival
October • 901-826-3629
www.riverartsfest.org

Memphis • Southeastern
Indian Folklife Festival
October • 901-785-3160

Memphis • Cooper-Young Festival
September • 901-276-7222
www.cooperyoungfestival.com

Milan • Fall Folklore Jamboree
October • 731-686-7362
www.milan.tennessee.edu

Monteagle • Fog Festival
February • 931-924-5353
www.monteaglechamber.com

Monteagle • Taste of the
Mountain Food Fair
March • www.monteaglechamber.com

Morristown • International Festival
April • 423-581-4330
www.rosecenter.org

Morristown • Blues, Soul
& BBQ Festival
June • 423-581-4330

Morristown • Mountain
Makins' Festival
October • 423-581-4330
www.rosecenter.org

Morristown • Great Smoky
Mountain Fall Festival
September • 865-993-2977
www.nhcvfd.com

Moss • Brimstock Bluegrass Festival
April • 931-258-4499

Mountain City • Pumpkin Festival
October • 423-246-5483

Murfreesboro
Uncle Dave Macon Days
July • 1-800-716-7560
www.uncledavemacondays.com

Murfreesboro
International Folk Fest
June • 615-896-3559
www.mboro-international-folkfest.org

Murfreesboro
American Indian Festival
March • 615-796-4210
www.mtsu.edu/powwow

Murfreesboro • Jazzfest
May • 615-895-1887
www.mainstreetjazzfest.com

Nashville • Nashville Film Festival
April • www.nashvillefilmfestival.org

Nashville • CMA Music Festival
June • 1-800-CMA-FEST (262-3378)
www.cmafest.com

Nashville • American Artisan Festival
June • 615-298-4691

Nashville • Jefferson Street
Jazz & Blues Festival
June • 615-726-5867
www.jumptojefferson.com

Nashville • Crawfish Boil Nashville
May • www.nashvillecrawfishboil.com

Nashville • Biscuits and
Bluegrass Fall Festival
October • 615-646-9700
www.lovelesscafe.com

Nashville • Bluegrass Fan Fest
October • 888-438-4262

Nashville • Germantown's
Oktoberfest
October • 615-818-3959
www.nashvilleoktoberfest.com

Nashville • Music & Molasses Festival
October • www.tnagmuseum.org

Nashville • Tennessee History Festival
October • 615-741-5280

Nashville • African Street Festival
September • 615-251-0007
www.aacanashville.org

Nashville Shores • A Toast to
Tennessee Wine Festival
May • 615-758-3478
www.atoasttotennessee.com

Norris • Anvil Shoot and Celebration
July • 865-494-7680
www.museumofappalachia.org

Norris • Tennessee Fall Homecoming
October • 865-494-7680
www.museumofappalachia.com

Oak Ridge • International Festival
February • 865-482-1074
www.childrensmuseumofoakridge.org

Oak Ridge • Secret City Festival
June • 866-506-6285
www.secretcityfestival.com

October • Southern Festival of Books
Nashville • 615-770-0006
www.tn-humanities.org/festival/

Tennessee

Oliver Springs
Historical Society Fall Festival
November • 865-435-2509
www.oshistorical.com

Paris • World's Biggest Fish Fry
April • 731-644-1143
www.paristnchamber.com

Parsons • Peavine Arts
& Crafts Festival
September • 731-847-6358
www.cityofparsons.com

Pigeon Forge • Saddle Up
February • 1-800-251-9100
www.mypigeonforge.com

Pigeon Forge • Appalachiafest
January • 800-251-9100
www.mypigeonforge.com

Pigeon Forge • DollyWood KidsFest
June • 800-DOLLYWOOD
www.dollywood.com

Pigeon Forge • A Mountain Quiltfest
March • 1-800-251-9100
www.mountainquiltfest.com

Pigeon Forge • Festival of Nations
March • 800-DOLLYWOOD
www.dollywood.com

Pigeon Forge • Winterfest Kickoff
November • 800-251-9100
www.mypigeonforge.com/winterfest.asp

Pigeon Forge • National
Gospel & Harvest Celebration
October • 800-DOLLYWOOD
www.dollywood.com

Pigeon Forge • Barbecue &
Bluegrass Festival
September • 800-DOLLYWOOD
www.dollywood.com

Pikeville • Log Cabin Days
May • 423-533-2732
www.southeasttennessee.com

Pikeville • Bledsoe
Fall Harvest Festival
October • www.pikevillefestival.com

Pikeville • Mountaineer Folk Festival
September • 800-250-8611
www.fallcreekfalls.org/currentevents.html

Piney Flats • Woolly Day
April • 423-538-7396
www.rockymountmuseum.com

Portland • Middle Tennessee
Strawberry Festival
May • 615-325-9032
www.portlandtn.com

Pulaski • Giles County
Gobbler's Gala
April • 931-363-3789
www.gilescountytourism.com

Ripley • Lauderdale County
Tomato Festival
July • 731-635-9541
www.lctn.com/tomato-festival

Roan Mountain
Rhododendron Festival
June • 800-250-8620
www.roanmountain.com/festival.htm

Rock City • Rocktoberfest
October • 800-854-0675
www.seerockcity.com

Rockwood • Family Fall Festival
October • 800-FUN-IN-TN
www.roanealliance.org

Rutledge • Grainger County
Tomato Festival
July • 865-828-4480
www.graingercountytomatofestival.com

Selmer • Hockaday
Broomcorn Festival
September • 731-645-6360
www.tast.tn.org

Selmer • VillageFest
September • 888-849-5344
www.rcvvillagefest.com

Sevierville • Bloomin'
Barbeque & Bluegrass
May • 888-766-5948
www.bloominbbq.com

Sevierville • Winterfest Kick Off
November • 888-738-4378
www.visitsevierville.com

Shady Valley • Cranberry Festival
October • 739-2131 or 727-5800

Shelbyville • Great Celebration
Mule & Donkey Show
July • 931-684-5915
www.twhnc.com

Smithville • Fiddler's
Jamboree & Crafts Festival
July • 615-597-8500
www.smithvillejamboree.com

Smyrna • Tennessee Heritage
BBQFestival
June • 615-459-2341
www.tennesseeheritagebarbecuefestival.com

Somerville • Fayette County
Cotton Festival
September • 901-465-8690
www.cottonfestivaltn.com

South Pittsburg • National
Cornbread Festival
April • 423-837-0022
www.nationalcornbread.com

South Pittsburg • Sweetens
Cove Country Festival
October • 423-837-7846

Spencer • Mountain Homecoming
July • 931-946-7461

Summertown • Bluegrass Festival
August • 931-964-2100

Tellico Plains • Harvest Festival
September • 888-562-4711
www.monroecounty.com

Tiptonville
Reelfoot Lake Eagle Festival
February • 888-313-8366
www.reelfoottourism.com

Tiptonville
Reelfoot Arts & Crafts Festival
October • 731-885-7295
www.reelfootartsandcrafts.com

Townsend • Winter Heritage
Festival in the Smokies
February • 800-525-6834
www.smokymountainfestivals.org

Townsend • Smoky Mountain
Pottery Festival
June • 800-525-6834
www.smokymountainfestivals.org

Townsend • Spring Heritage Festival
May • 865-448-0044
www.gsmheritagecenter.org

Townsend • Heritage Festival
and Old Timers Day
September • 1-800-525-6834
www.smokymountains.org

Trenton • Teapot Festival
May • 731-855-2013
www.teapotcollection.com

Tullahoma • Arts and Crafts Festival
May • 931.455.1234
www.tullahomafinearts.org

Unicoi • Fiddlers &
Fiddleheads Festival
April • 423-743-8799
www.farmhousegallery.net

Vonore • Great Island Festival
& 18th Century Trade Faire
September • 423-884-6246
www.sequoyahmuseum.org

Wartburg • Morgan County
Octoberfest Music Festival
October • 423-346-5740
www.morgancountychamber.com

Watertown • Jazz Festival
& Excursion Train
July • 615-237-9338
www.visitwilsoncounty.com

Waverly • Autumn Blaze Arts Festival
October • 931-296-5860

Waynesboro • Pumpkin
Harvest Festival
October • 931-722-5458
www.waynecountychamber.org

White Bluff • Apple Butter Festival
October • 615-797-3409
www.dicksoncountychamber.com

White Bluff • Main Street Festival
October • 615-797-3131
www.townofwhitebluff.com

White House • Harvest Moon Festival
October • 615-672-2265
www.sumnercvb.com

Winchester • International
Dogwood Festival
May • 866-967-2532
www.winchesterdogwoodfestival.com

Winfield • Appalachian
Dumplin' Festival
May • 423-569-6139
www.appalachiandumplinfestival.com

Woodbury • Good Ole Days
in Cannon County
May • 615-563-5518

Index

Q

292 Recipes for 30 Varieties of Game

The sportsman's outdoor experience doesn't end when the gun or the fishing gear has been put away. The challenge and reward of the quest are continued when the game is prepared into fabulous meals to be shared with friends and family.

Veteran hunter, fisherman, and chef Harold Webster delights sportsmen and those who cook game with seasonal recipes for venison, fish, fowl, and other delicacies from field and water. Fans of Webster's wild-game cookbooks and his popular newspaper column will recognize his trademark recipe clarity and his expert advice on handling, preparing, and serving game.

In addition to the recipes, Webster tells fascinating stories about the capturing, cleaning and cooking of the game. Stories like ***Bow Season: Best Deer Hunt of the Year***, ***Come Gather at Our Table***, ***Stalking the Wild Fall Turkey***, and ***Poochie was a Feist Dog*** make this book an entertaining read as well as an essential resource for creating memorable meals from any hunter's bounty.

Game for All Seasons
$16.95 • 240 pp • 7 x 10
paperbound

Also available from Great American Publishers:

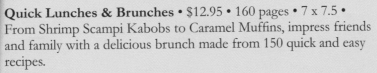

900 recipes make up this outstanding collection created with the everyday cook in mind. Each cookbook features 150 easy-to-prepare recipes using common ingredients that are easily found in your local grocery store (most will already be in your kitchen!).

Quick Crockery Cooking • $12.95 • 160 pages • 7 x 7.5 • You'll be in and out of the kitchen fast with creative crockery recipes that are easy, economical and DELICIOUS.

Quick Desserts • $12.95 • 160 pages • 7 x 7.5 • Get out of the kitchen and into the fun with more than 150 recipes for the best-tasting desserts of all time.

Quick Hors d'oeuvres • $12.95 • 160 pages • 7 x 7.5 • Entertaining friends and family is a snap with quick and easy recipes for all-time favorite hors d'oeuvres and beverages.

Quick Lunches & Brunches • $12.95 • 160 pages • 7 x 7.5 • From Shrimp Scampi Kabobs to Caramel Muffins, impress friends and family with a delicious brunch made from 150 quick and easy recipes.

Quick Mexican Cooking • $12.95 • 160 pages • 7 x 7.50 • More than 150 quick and easy recipes for meal after meal of pure Mexican pleasure.

Quick Soups 'n Salads • $12.95 • 160 pages • 7 x 7.5 • Preparing delicious, nutritious soups and salads has never been easier.

State Hometown Cookbook Series
Collect Them All!

Each title in the HOMETOWN COOKBOOK SERIES contains FAVORITE recipes from Hometowns all over the state plus fun side-bars featuring food festivals throughout the state. This series is great for anyone who loves to cook, cookbook collectors, and armchair travelers. $16.95 each.

If not available locally, use the order form below, or call us toll-free 1.888.854.5954 or visit us on the web at

www.GreatAmericanPublishers.com

- - ✂ -

Order Form MAIL TO: Great American Publishers • P. O. Box 1305 • Kosciusko, MS 39090

❑ Check Enclosed

Charge to: ❑ Visa ❑ MC ❑ AmEx ❑ Disc

Card# _____

Exp Date _____ Signature _____

Name _____

Address _____

City _____ State _____ Zip _____

Phone _____

Email _____

Qty. Title _____ Total _____

_____ _____ _____
_____ _____ _____
_____ _____ _____
_____ _____ _____
_____ _____ _____
_____ _____ _____
_____ _____ _____

Subtotal _____
Postage ($3 1st book; $.50 each additional) _____
Total _____

248 ·

Tennessee